Three Fartown

Hunter, Cooper, ~~Devery~~

David Gronow

London League Publications Ltd

Three Fartown Aussies
Hunter, Cooper, Devery

© David Gronow. Foreword © Maurice Oldroyd

The moral right of David Gronow to be identified as the author has been asserted.

Cover design © Stephen McCarthy.

Front cover: The 1953 Huddersfield team after winning the Challenge Cup at Wembley. Back cover: The 1948–49 Huddersfield team that won the Championship.

All photographs in this book are from private collections unless otherwise credited. No copyright has been intentionally breached; please contact London League Publications Ltd if you believe there has been a breach of copyright.

A CIP catalogue record for this book is available from the British Library.

First published in Great Britain in May 2012 by:
London League Publications Ltd, P.O. Box 65784, London NW2 9NS

ISBN: 978-1903659-62-5

Cover design by: Stephen McCarthy Graphic Design
                                       46, Clarence Road, London N15 5BB

Layout: Peter Lush

Printed and bound in Great Britain by Charlesworth Press, Wakefield

Foreword

I am indeed indebted to David Gronow for giving me this opportunity to ignite a few memories about my all-time Fartown favourites. My earliest memory of the stadium is of playing in a curtain-raiser at Fartown for Birkby School at the age of nine. I also remember going to watch Leeds play Wakefield at Fartown in the 1947 Challenge Cup semi-final. The crowd was a Fartown record of 35,000, and I got in at half-time (when admission was free) after having been to see a *Flash Gordon* film first.

Fartown also holds so many memories of the game at professional level, not least the great Huddersfield side which included such as Pat Devery, Lionel Cooper and Johnny Hunter.

There was the 1949 Championship Final when 75,000 saw Huddersfield beat Warrington 13–12 at Maine Road, Manchester, and the official referee, Mr Smith of Barrow, didn't turn up because of a breakdown in communications – Matt Coates took over from the touchline, and the rest was history.

Huddersfield has always been a much respected club, and after the Second World War ended they set out their search to attract top players from all corners of the globe. The game of rugby league was given a tremendous boost when the 1946 England team, the 'Indomitables', toured Australia and New Zealand – this successful tour ensured that many of the world's top players were put in the shop window for all to see.

The club, to their credit, lost no time in securing Lionel Cooper and Johnny Hunter, and leaving seeds to germinate for Pat Devery to follow – a great stroke of business for all concerned.

Johnny Hunter was a flamboyant, devil-may-care footballer who changed the whole style of full back play which was, at that time, long-kicking duels to gain ground advantage. Full-backs like Jimmy Ledgard and Freddie Miller were masters of that style of play – these duels were like tennis matches with 'head turning' at each kick until someone dropped the ball or gained ground by launching the ball into touch. Hunter played the 'extra back' to perfection – the big kicks he received he would catch on the run, often with one hand reaching over the touchline.

Norman Wainwright – Hunter's centre at the time – recalls in a game at Hunslet, Hunter caught the ball in the in-goal area by the corner flag, and stayed in the in-goal area as he ran across until he met the goalpost. With his non-ball carrying hand he swivelled around the post at 90 degrees, wrong-footed everybody and then ran the length of the field, beating man after man and scored a sensational try.

Lionel Cooper was without doubt one of the most outstanding wingers in the history of the game. His powerful frame and robust running style was an awesome sight to any would-be tacklers, but pleasurable to the home spectators in particular.

As a youngster I thought that professional sportsmen on the rugby field were fearless, but I was proven wrong. In one match, Lionel was in full flow and going for the corner flag, with a powerful visiting forward coming across to cover tackle him – suddenly as I watched the tacklers face it dawned on him he was going to cut-off Lionel, but I could see the terror in his eyes, he slowed down and dived behind Cooper – a clear case of self-preservation.

Pat Devery was a classic runner, poetry in motion. When I used to go in the score box behind the posts I had the best elevated view of anybody in the ground. When Fartown won a scrum the ball went from Billy Banks to Peter Ramsden to Russ Pepperell then to Devery.

When Pat threw his head back a roar of expectancy came from the whole crowd who were all on their toes – waiting for Lionel to receive his pass from Devery and 'do his stuff' – and he didn't disappoint that often.

The Fartown style was simply 13-man rugby – to entertain spectators and win trophies. Long may that continue with the present day Giants.

Maurice Oldroyd
Patron of BARLA

Maurice Oldroyd has given a lifetime's service to rugby league, especially BARLA and the amateur game. He is a lifelong Huddersfield supporter.

Lionel Cooper and Johnny Hunter.

Acknowledgements

In compiling this book invaluable help has been provided by other writers on the game of rugby league – most notably, Robert Gate – whose knowledge of rugby league knows no bounds, David Middleton (League Information Services, Australia), Ian Heads and Sean Fagan (Australia).

Obtaining the material in this book has involved a great deal of assistance from others who have been generous in providing pictures and information – the *Huddersfield Examiner*, Michelle Nielsen (Projects Manager, Balmain Tigers Rugby League Club), Ingrid Piper (Your Say Editor: *Sydney Daily Herald*), Gary Lester, publisher of *From Where the Sun Rises, 100 Years of the Sydney Roosters*, Harry Edgar, Publisher/Editor of the *Rugby League Journal*, and the *Huddersfield Examiner* archive at Huddersfield Library.

I must also acknowledge "Autolycus" (Sidney H. Crowther of the *Huddersfield Examiner*), E.E. Christensen's *Rugby League Yearbook for 1947, Tiger, Tiger Burning Bright - the story of Balmain Rugby League Club* by Ray Chesterman, the testimonial books *Johnny* and *Lionel* compiled by A.N. Gaulton, the *Rugby League Gazette* and *Rugby League Review* published by Stanley Chadwick.

Many of the photographs in this book are from private collections; if copyrights have been infringed it is without intent.

Special thanks go to Pat Devery, Glenn and Jan Hunter (son and daughter of Johnny), Reg Cooper (younger brother of Lionel), Maurice Oldroyd – for his personal recollections of three great players, and fond reminisces by Huddersfield rugby league supporters, Diane Beaumont Armitage, James Dyson, Margaret Mullany and Raymond Prior, who were kind enough to contact me with memories of days gone by, and to David Thorpe for helping with cricketing memories.

David Gronow
Huddersfield
April 2012

London League Publications Ltd would like to thank Steve McCarthy for designing the cover, Michael O'Hare – a lifelong Fartown supporter – for sub-editing the book, and the staff of Charlesworth Press for printing it.

About the author

David Gronow was born and bred in Huddersfield, and still lives in the town. He is the grandson of Fartown great Ben Gronow, one of the club's heroes from the Northern Union era.

Currently club historian of Huddersfield Giants Rugby League Club, Rugby League has always been part of David's life. He has always supported Fartown, now the Giants, and the first Wembley Final he attended was in 1962. He recalls that after being beaten by Wakefield Trinity at Wembley, Huddersfield beat Trinity at Odsal to win the Championship. He remembers that team as having a great pack, expertly marshalled by Tommy Smales at scrum-half.

His father and uncles also played for Huddersfield, and he helped form works side David Brown Gears ARL who joined the Pennine League in Division Five in 1977–78 after playing in the end of season Fartown Workshops Competition.

He served as secretary of Huddersfield Rugby League Club Players Association for going on 15 years, and is actively involved on a Steering Committee in a Heritage Lottery Funded Project to safeguard the legacy of Huddersfield Rugby League. Celebrating 150 years of rugby in the town, this unique history will be collated and preserved through the project: *Huddersfield Rugby League: A Lasting Legacy.*

In the last few years he has had two books published on the club's history:

100 Greats: Huddersfield Rugby League Football Club (2008) and *Images of Huddersfield Rugby League Club* (2010).

David was also a keen cricketer for many years in the Huddersfield Cricket League, playing for Rastrick, Armitage Bridge and Golcar.

England or Great Britain?

Readers may query as to why the 'Indomitables' of 1946 were not under the heading of 'Great Britain' and were known as 'England', even though there were players of Welsh nationality on the tour.

In international rugby league the team was The Northern Union (1908 to 1922), England (1924 to 1946) and Great Britain (1947 to 2007).

The Rugby Football League decided that from 2008 onwards Great Britain would no longer be known as such, and that players would be able to represent England, Wales, Scotland and Ireland at test level.

Contents

Poetry

The achievements of Lionel Cooper and Johnny Hunter were recorded in poems by Brian Donaldson.

The Mighty Lionel

Who is this man called Cooper,
This man all wingers fear,
This man who's always dangerous
Whenever he gets near?

This sturdy-built Australian,
Since visiting our shores,
Has proved to be a man of power,
A man for making scores.

Every team opposing him
Are put into the "blue,"
Not one of them who plays to-day
Can this big man subdue.

We know just how to deal with him,"
They all say that at first,
But he's quite difficult to stop
When once he's on the burst.

Opposing wingmen make their vows
That he'll not score again,
But, somehow, it's beyond their powers,
Their efforts seem in vain.

Half of the team can wait for him,
He is afraid of none.
It's nothing new to see him cross
With three men hanging on.

If they decide to tackle him
By going for his knees
Just when they think they've got him taped
He'll hand them off with ease.

But these are not the only ways
In which he scores his tries.
His side-step baffles many teams
And takes them by surprise

Who is this man called Cooper?
Spectators well might ask,
The man who has to keep him marked
Receives no easy task.

Exhilarating Johnny

When Johnny Hunter plays full-back
He likes to join in the attack.
He enjoys every match he plays
And has exhilarating ways.

He is one of the happy sort
Who's good at almost any sport;
He's entertaining on his day
And that's where his attraction lay.

He came with Cooper over here
And soon the crowds began to cheer.
His first game was at Hull K.R
There one could see he was a star.

To him there is no greater fun
Than when he makes a zig-zag run;
He races down the field "all out,"
That he enjoys it there's no doubt.

Then, very often, if he can,
He comes and makes the extra man
To turn a move into a score;
And this has brought him tries galore.

Sometimes, if Johnny's in a fix,
He'll use one of his long range kicks
And follow up to take his man
Or gain possession if he can.

Besides his own abilities
He has his little "oddities,"
And one to which he's quite devout
Is that of coming "last man out."

Now Johnny's playing in the "Threes;'
His Fartown followers to please.
His burst is making many tries
And proving his selection wise.

He's always liked to keep in trim
But injuries have haunted him.
Though he's been often out of luck
He's always come again with pluck.

Let's hope he'll have a few years yet,
Crowned with success he won't forget.
Then, when he's finished his career,
He'll not forget his visit here.

1. The Australians are coming

The distinctive claret and gold strip of the Huddersfield Rugby League club came to the fore in the late 1940s and early 1950s. They won the League Championship in 1949 when Fartown – as the team were nicknamed after their historic ground – beat Warrington 13–12 in the final at Maine Road in front of, what was at the time a world-record crowd of 75,194. It was the climax of a season which had also brought home the Yorkshire League title.

The highest attendance at Fartown to watch a Huddersfield game was in the following season, 32,912 against Wigan on 4 March 1950. More success followed that season as Huddersfield retained the Yorkshire League title and reached another Championship Final at Maine Road.

By the end of the 1950s Huddersfield had won the Yorkshire Cup three times, in 1950–51, 1952–53 and 1957–58, and the Challenge Cup in 1952–53, when they beat St Helens 15–10 in the final at Wembley. But how did this success come about?

After 21 years of peace, the prospects at Fartown for the 1939–40 season were distinctly good, but the face of the world changed when German forces crossed the border into Poland, starting the Second World War.

Huddersfield's league fixtures had begun in August with victory at Swinton on the 26th, but in the following midweek game at Hull, the Fartowners lost 13–9. However, this lapse was soon forgotten when Featherstone Rovers visited Fartown on 2 September and were soundly beaten 56–10.

The next day, the country was at war with Germany. Prime Minister Neville Chamberlain addressed the nation on the radio at 11am, after failing to achieve anything by diplomatic means. Soon after the declaration of war, every man between the ages of 19 and 41 was called up for some kind of national service. Many women were also involved in the war effort, in the forces, on the land or in factory jobs that had previously been done by men.

This was followed shortly by an order from the Home Office that all places of entertainment and sports grounds be closed; no large crowds were to be allowed in congested areas for fear of enemy air attack. However, the government soon realised that, for both the civilian population and the armed forces, leisure activity was important to keep up morale and permission was soon granted for organised sport to continue on a limited basis.

There was no rugby at Fartown on 9 September, but a friendly was arranged with Hunslet. The New Zealand tourists, who were 12,000 miles from home and about to embark on a test series, had opened their tour at St Helens on 2 September, but as a result of U-boat activity in the Atlantic, decided to return home, but not before they had played, and won, a second match at Dewsbury.

The Rugby Football League (RFL) resolved to continue competitive rugby and formed a War Emergency League. The clubs played in separate Yorkshire and Lancashire sections to reduce the need for travel. The RFL also decided that professional players would be paid 10 shillings per match, including expenses.

After Huddersfield's Christmas games with Halifax, two months elapsed before weather conditions made further play possible, but the team finished second in the league.

The second season of wartime football brought many difficulties for Huddersfield, and if it had not been for the introduction of 'guest' players from the Lancashire clubs, it was doubtful whether a team could have been got together.

Many players were on active service, but were still able to make themselves available for other clubs on the proviso they had permission. Some clubs, including Wigan, Swinton and Salford, had their grounds closed down for use as military bases. A match between Hull and Batley was abandoned because of an air raid.

In 1940–41, a total of 46 players turned out for Huddersfield, with 24 guests from other clubs. In 1942–43, Huddersfield reached the final of the Yorkshire Cup, only to lose 7–2 on aggregate in the two games with Dewsbury. This was the club's15th appearance in a Yorkshire Cup final, their sixth as runners-up, otherwise the season was uneventful.

With an eye on the team's future needs, the Huddersfield committee signed several new players in the 1943–44 season. Jeff Bawden and Albert Pepperell were the most notable, but with military call-ups and an ongoing process of team-building, no cups were won. However, Russ Pepperell and Bill (W.T.) Davies were selected for the England versus Wales international.

In 1944–45, the last season of wartime rugby, Alex Fiddes led Huddersfield to victory against Bradford Northern in the Challenge Cup Final. The first leg was played in a blizzard at Fartown and ended with a 7–4 victory for Huddersfield. In the second leg at Odsal, on 5 May 1945, the Fartowners asserted their authority with a 6–5 victory, making the aggregate score 13–9. It was the fifth time the Cup had come to Fartown.

Things were beginning to change, hostilities were coming to a close, and the RFL celebrated their jubilee in the 1945–46 season. They also made a significant decision to tour Australia and New Zealand in 1946. The achievements of that five month tour would go down in rugby league history. In Australia, the war years had produced large crowds and, financially at least, the sport did not appear to suffer the hardships it had endured in the First World War. Nonetheless, the loss of young men away fighting weakened the pool of talent available.

The years following the Second World War were undoubtedly a sporting golden age, not just for rugby league, but also for the Huddersfield club and the 1945–46 season saw something like normality returning to the sport.

Enthusiasm was sky high, and the sport's affluence in a time of austerity was highlighted by a merry-go-round of transfers for large fees and huge crowds. In the first full season after the war, Huddersfield sold Bill Davies to Dewsbury for £1,650, then a record, but this figure was exceeded five times in the next two seasons.

The sport was boosted by the 1946 Rugby League Lions 'Indomitables' tour which marked the relaunch of international rugby league in a world which had been devastated by the war. The Lions retained the Ashes and became the only British team to remain unbeaten in a full test series in Australia.

A further reason for the massive increase in crowds and interest in the sport was the overseas players who came to play in British rugby league. The 1937 ban on international transfers had expired during the war. The RFL had been more than willing to renew it after the war and the 1946 British tour managers, Walter Popplewell of Batley and Barrow's Wilf Gabbatt, approached the Australian Board of Control to discuss the subject. However, the Australian clubs had healthy bank balances, but a dearth of talent in their own country, and so completely reversed their previous position. They fully expected members of Gus Risman's Lions squad to return to Australia, but none did.

In the meantime, British clubs took full advantage of Australia's decision, and many top players decided to try their luck in England, a year after the end of the 1946 Lions tour.

Australia, shocked by what was happening, decided belatedly, to demand a new five-year ban on British clubs signing Australian and New Zealand rugby league players. This was agreed by the Rugby League Council in August 1947, but it was too late to stop players who had already signed for English clubs coming to England.

The exodus of players of both codes joining English clubs at that time included Arthur Clues, a forward from Wests, Ted Verrenkamp, a centre from Souths in Brisbane, Frank Cottle, a centre from North Sydney, plus Jack Niddrie and Len Kenny, both wingers, from North Sydney and Valleys Brisbane respectively, who all joined at Leeds.

George Watt, the Australian test hooker, arrived at Hull from Eastern Suburbs. He moved to Humberside after playing with New South Wales country club Boorowa in 1947. Bruce Ryan, a wingman from Newtown, also joined Hull, along with half-back Duncan Jackson from Sydney's Northern Suburbs rugby union club.

Don Graham, a stand-off from St George joined Hunslet, while Bob Bartlett, a centre, arrived at Bramley from Wollongong. Denis Boocker, a centre from West Wyalong joined Wakefield Trinity, and John (Jeff) McGilvray, the Adelong full-back, accepted an offer to join Workington Town. Harry Bath joined Barrow, but soon moved on to Warrington, where he linked up with fellow Australian Brian Bevan. New Zealander Ces Mountford signed for Wigan, and went on to become one of the club's post-war greats.

Last, but not least, Johnny Hunter, who played at full-back, and Lionel Cooper, the Australian test wingman, both arrived at Huddersfield from Eastern Suburbs, together with Pat Devery, the Australian and Balmain stand-off. Dave Hadfield, in *Playing Away*, a history of Australian players in British rugby league, said that "What was clear in England in 1947 was that Australia had closed the stable door after the horse – and a thoroughbred at that – had bolted. And nobody had derived more benefit from the delay than those accomplished rustlers at Huddersfield."

The scene was set, and so began one of the most successful eras in Huddersfield Rugby League Club's history.

* * * * *

Australian players have been gracing the British rugby league scene for more than100 years. After the first Kangaroo tour of 1908–09, Albert Rosenfeld (Huddersfield), Jim Devereux (Hull), Mick Bolewski (Leigh), Syd Deane (Oldham), Dan Frawley and Larry O'Malley, both at Warrington, all decided to throw in their lot with English clubs.

The desire to build the strongest teams available by recruiting players from far and wide was nothing new to rugby league clubs. The need to increase both attendances and playing standards was of paramount importance. Huddersfield was certainly no different to other clubs at that time. The determination of the Fartown committee to still further strengthen their team was responsible for Thomas Patrick Gleeson making a 6,000 mile journey to join the club. Gleeson was signed from Glebe in Australia in November 1912.He became Harold Wagstaff's co-centre; and it was with Gleeson as his centre that Rosenfeld set up his try-scoring record of 80 in a season.

In an effort to encourage local talent, the Northern Union committee decided at a meeting in Huddersfield on 11 February 1913 that no player who had played in New Zealand or Australia should in future be allowed to play professional rugby league in England, unless a two-year residential period in England had been completed.

The residential qualification was removed in 1923, but re-imposed after a few weeks following a protest by the New South Wales League. The ban on players from down under remained in force until 9 June 1927, when, by 20 votes to 9, the RFL Council decided to cancel the agreement. Within a few hours of the decision being announced, the Huddersfield club officials had secured the signature of the Australian threequarter Ernest Mills.

In Australia, Mills had played for the Grenfell team coached by former Huddersfield star Ben Gronow. Tremendously quick, he was a member of the Huddersfield side which won the Championship in 1928–29 and 1929–30, and was a Challenge Cup winner in 1933 when Huddersfield beat Warrington 21–17 at Wembley. Mills played 336 times for the Fartowners, scored 290 tries and kicked 23 goals.

In 1931, in response to the appeals of the New South Wales, Queensland and New Zealand Leagues, it was agreed by the RFL that if any club in England signed 'first or second grade players' from these three leagues, they should pay £200 compensation 'to an authority to be named by them'.

After 10 years freedom of action, the Rugby League Council re-imposed the ban on colonial players, together with the two year residential qualification. Huddersfield, who had signed the first player when the ban was lifted, were also the last to secure two Australians, Ron Bailey and Tom Grahame. The agreement lapsed at the end of 1941, and was not renewed.

Another player who had made the long trip to England was Ray Markham, who was from Wollongong and played for Cessnock, just west of Newcastle in New South Wales (NSW). He arrived in Huddersfield on 31 December 1932, and within four months had a Challenge Cup winners' medal in his grasp. He played on the opposite wing to Ernie Mills.

Markham went on to score 255 tries and kick three goals in 263 appearances for the club. He stayed in England after retiring at the end of the 1938–39 season, when he was appointed superintendent of Huddersfield Corporation Markets and Fairs Department. He moved to Derby, served in the RAF in the Second World War and then came back to Yorkshire to settle in Bradford, where he lived until his death in 1988.

In the late 1940s and early 1950s, enterprise and a fixed determination to develop Huddersfield into an all-star combination meant that it was not going to be easy to fit in all the players who were available. In the late 1940s there was increased activity in rugby league both to find new players and transfers between clubs. Huddersfield had captured the Australian trio of Hunter, Cooper and Devery, and had also gone to South Africa for rugby union players. Ian Clark and Kenneth Morrison, who were both originally from Bulawayo, Southern Rhodesia, signed for Huddersfield in January 1948.

The Fartown club was becoming quite cosmopolitan in character. Its ranks included three Australians, three Welshmen, three Scots and two Rhodesians. There had been a time before the war when Wigan had been dubbed 'Other Nationalities', but that distinction had now been shouldered by Huddersfield.

Huddersfield had also recruited from junior clubs in Cumberland before the formation of professional clubs in that area, notably Jeff Bawden and Bob Nicholson from Hensingham and Russ Pepperell from Seaton. Unusually for professional rugby league, the club's regular first team line ups of that period did not include a single local born player.

In the early part of 1947, there was both elation and mystification among Huddersfield's followers. There was elation at the announcement that Lionel Cooper had been signed. The mystification was at the news that the move was a 'double deal', and that a full-back named Johnny Hunter was to accompany Cooper to Fartown.

Who on earth was Johnny Hunter?

2. Hunter and Cooper arrive

John Cheyne Hugh Hunter was born on 21 July 1926, in the Sydney suburb of Kogarah, New South Wales. He was educated at schools run by the Catholic Marist Brothers, first at Kogarah then at the Greater Public School (GPS) St Joseph's College, Hunters Hill, where he excelled at sport. He played centre for three years in the rugby union first team, coached by the legendary Brother Henry, and for the cricket first eleven.

At the time there was sibling rivalry with his younger brother Ken, who like Johnny was a good all-round sportsman. Ken also played first team for St Josephs, and went on to play for Eastern Suburbs in 1949 and from 1951 to 1954.

The brothers were both accomplished boxers. Johnny won a trophy in the under-16 year group for best 'scientific' boxer, while Ken was more the 'Rocky Marciano' type and became heavyweight champion of the Australian Occupational Forces in Japan in 1947.

Johnny Hunter's son Glenn recalled: "Grandfather had a system for resolving disputes between the two boys – a makeshift ring and two sets of boxing gloves."

After leaving school, Hunter worked as a furniture salesman and joined the Australian Army in 1943.Although this was still wartime, he was not deployed overseas and served his time out at the Randwick Racecourse Army Camp.

While in the Army, Hunter became a close friend of Ray Lindwall, who already had a huge reputation as a cricket fast bowler, and was an accomplished rugby league full-back for St George. He played in the 1942 and 1946 Premiership Finals. In 1948, Lindwall achieved legendary status in cricket when he was selected for the Ashes tour of England with Don Bradman's 'Invincibles'.[1]

Hunter's first foray into senior rugby was with the Drummoyne District rugby union club, before he changed codes and joined the Eastern Suburbs rugby league club. He made his debut against Newtown at Sydney Cricket Ground on 21 April 1945.

Hunter had received quite a few tips about full-back play from Lindwall, and his improvement was such that in his first season in the Sydney competition he was considered for a test place against the 1946 touring England team, but his chances were ruined by a knee injury.

Still, adequate compensation was on the way when Huddersfield's

---

[1] Some of the information about Hunter's life in Australia is from *Johnny*, his testimonial booklet.

offer came, however, the call was for Lionel Cooper, who had established himself playing for Eastern Suburbs, New South Wales and Australia.

The famous Australian centre, Dinny Campbell, who was then acting as agent for Leeds, offered a four-year contract to Cooper to come to Headingley. Cooper insisted that the contract should be for three years and would only move to England if his friend and Easts team-mate, full-back Johnny Hunter, who had not gained any representative honours, but had played alongside Cooper in Easts' 1945 Premiership Final winning side against Balmain, could come with him. He did not want to travel to England on his own. Easts had also won the minor premiership in 1945 – their seventh in 13 seasons – and had finished one point ahead of Newtown.

Leeds wanted Cooper, but were hesitant at the prospect of signing a relatively unknown player in Hunter, hence negotiations broke down. Huddersfield grasped this opportunity with both hands and stepped in to sign Cooper, together with Johnny Hunter. The latter had played 21 times for Easts and scored five tries.

The detail of the story is that journalist Eddie Waring had been responsible for a lot of players coming to British rugby league, in particular quite a few from Australia. In 1947, after he had been to Australia on the 1946 tour working for the *Sunday Pictorial* he was asked by Huddersfield if he could help them get an Australian player.

Huddersfield gave Waring a free hand and he told them that it would cost £1,500 to get Cooper and another player. Waring's Australian contact, Ray Stehr said they could get Johnny Hunter, who was 'an adventurous full-back'. Waring had remembered seeing Hunter in reserve grade rugby. He liked his stylish play and cabled Stehr "Sign Cooper and Hunter for £1500".

Lionel William Cooper was born on 18 February 1922, in West Wyalong, which is located in the Central West Region of New South Wales. He was a pupil at Cowra High School in the Lachlan Valley, and although Cooper broke no records in the scholastic department, he did represent his school at cricket, tennis and, surprisingly, association football, which was very much the smallest of the football codes at that time in Australia.[2]

As a small boy between the ages of two and five he spent three years blind, having incurred 'sandy blight' which is an acute form of eye inflammation. This required occasional treatment throughout his career.

---

[2] The information about Cooper's early life is from *Lionel*, his testimonial booklet.

After leaving school at the age of 13, he found his sport was limited to cricket on Saturday mornings. This remained so until he moved from the country to live in Sydney in 1937, where the family residence was directly opposite the Enfield Olympic Swimming Pool. His attention turned to swimming in the summer months and tennis in the winter, until he joined the Australian Infantry Forces in 1942.

Army life gave him the ideal opportunity to play cricket and participate in athletics. In September 1943, he was briefly posted to the north of Australia, before he returned to Conclurry in Queensland, where, in one afternoon in an Army and Air Force Sports competition, he won the 75-yard, 100-yard and 220-yard sprints, and came second to Don Chadwick, the New Zealand high jump record holder, in the long jump.

Early 1944 saw him return to Katherine in Northern Territory, where he joined a commando unit and subsequently changed the course of his life. As well as developing into a good all-round cricketer, his interest turned to Australian Rules Football in the winter months.

However, his army unit decided to form a rugby league team with a view to entering into a competition to be run in Northern Territory later in the season. Fate took a hand at an inter-service meeting in Darwin.

Cooper met the man who was to be his tutor and the man who introduced him to rugby league – Warrant Officer Ray Stehr. He was a former player who had toured England with Australia in 1933 and 1937.

In 1944, Stehr gave Cooper a try out at centre in an Army combined side to play a representative team from the Air Force, but Cooper seemed somewhat overawed by it all. Shortly after this he transferred to Wyndham on the north west coast of Australia, and left rugby behind.

In January 1945, after a period of leave at home in Sydney, he returned to camp at Liverpool, in NSW, where he was lined up on the parade ground in front of Sergeant Bill Dunn, who had been the referee in the match Cooper had played at the request of Ray Stehr. Dunn, together with Stehr and his former commanding officer, Major White, advised Cooper to revive his interest in rugby league.

At that time in Sydney, it was the norm that a person had to play for the club where they lived, through a residential qualification system. So because Cooper had previously lived in the Western Suburbs area, it was accepted that he would join Wests and asked for a trial. However, he was told that because he was still commandeered to the army with every possibility he could be transferred further afield, that he should return after the war if he was still interested.

Cooper returned to camp at Liverpool, and told Stehr of the situation.

At the same time he was told that his period of training was to be changed from signals to gunnery, which took three months, which gave him the chance of a possible trial with one of the other Sydney clubs.

Stehr was captain-coach of the Eastern Suburbs club, it was only natural that Cooper give Easts a go. In March 1945 he turned out on the Sydney Sports Ground for his first training night in plimsolls, army jersey and football shorts loaned to him by Stehr.

Eastern Suburbs (today called the Sydney Roosters) were founded at a meeting held at Paddington Town Hall on 24 January 1908 which decided that the district should enter a team in the newly-formed New South Wales Rugby Football League. They are the only club that has been ever-present in the Premiership.

Unofficially, they were known as the 'Tricolours' due to their red, white and blue jerseys, styled on the playing strip of the 1899 Great Britain rugby union team that toured Australia. In the Australians' first rugby league touring party to England and Wales in 1908–09 was Easts stand-off half Albert Aaron Rosenfeld. He signed for Huddersfield at the end of the tourists' game at Fartown on 20 February 1909 after Huddersfield had beaten Australia 5–3.

In 1913, Eastern Suburbs became the first club to win three consecutive Premierships and had amassed a team of outstanding talent. Their line-ups in this period included Dally Messenger, Harry 'Jersey' Flegg and Sandy Pearce, all rugby league greats. Ten of their players had represented Australia, another three had won New South Wales honours.

Easts missed the finals once from 1926 to 1942 and in that time won four titles and the minor premiership on seven occasions. In 1935 Easts lost just one game and recorded the highest winning margin in their history, an 87–7 victory over Canterbury, and headed the league table at the end of the season by a massive eight points.

In 1936 Easts became one of five teams in Premiership history to remain undefeated for an entire season, a feat they repeated the following year. Easts supplied eight players for the 1938 Kangaroo tour to England. In 1940, Easts, led by tough forward Ray Stehr, beat Canterbury with a 24–14 win in the Final, and the following season reached the Final, but lost 31–14 to St George.

Under Stehr's guidance and coaching, Cooper made his debut in the Eastern Suburbs side against Newtown at the Sydney Cricket Ground on 21 April 1945, alongside Johnny Hunter.

Hunter and Cooper played centre and wing respectively. Easts ended the season as minor Premiers. They won the Premiership Final against Balmain on 1 September at the Sydney Cricket Ground in front of a crowd of 44,585.

Balmain led 10–5 at the interval, and the match was evenly balanced throughout the second half. With three minutes remaining, Easts trailed 18–17 and received a penalty on halfway. Dick Dunn convinced his reluctant captain Ray Stehr that he could make the distance and successfully kicked the goal.

Dunn then received Joe Jorgenson's kick from the restart and booted the ball into touch five yards from the Balmain line. Easts hooker George Watt won the scrum against the feed and their classy half-back pairing of Sel Lisle and Wally O'Connell put a move on that saw Dunn score in the corner. Dunn scored 19 of Easts 22 points that day. He carried his 14-month old daughter's sock in his shorts pocket for luck throughout the match. The teams that day were:

Eastern Suburbs: Ray Pratt, Lionel Cooper, Paul Tierney, Johnny Hunter, Ken Foster, Wally O'Connell, Sel Lisle, Ray Stehr (c), George Watt, Jack Arnold, Bert Rollason, Sid Hobson, Dick Dunn. Coach: Arthur Halloway.
Scorers: Tries: Dunn 3, Arnold. Goals: Dunn 5.
Balmain: Dave Parkinson, Robert Nielsen, Joe Jorgenson, Tom Bourke (c), Robert Paterson, Harry Leo, Stan Ponchard, Jack Spencer, Ernie Dawes, Hilton Kidd, Jim Metcalf, Sid Ryan, Jack Hampstead. Coach: Norm Robinson.
Scorers: Tries: Ponchard 2, Dawes, Nielsen. Goals: Jorgenson 3.

August 1945 saw the cessation of hostilities and Lionel Cooper was posted to Victoria Barracks in Sydney, which enabled him to continue his rugby in the winter months of 1946.

He had the distinction of playing for New South Wales after only six games of first grade rugby, was Australia's outstanding player of 1946, and had the honour, along with Balmain's Joe Jorgenson, of being the only player in the State chosen for every representative match played.

He played for Sydney Firsts against Country Firsts, New South Wales against England twice, and scored two tries, New South Wales versus Queensland twice, again with two tries and all three test matches against England.

Cooper also toured Queensland with NSW and played against the state team at the Brisbane Cricket Ground, scoring one try, and against Wide Bay at Gympie, where he notched four tries in a 43–13 win. He wound up the year playing for a Combined Sydney side in a charity match against the NSW Police.

One of the closest and most thrilling matches in which the 1946 Lions were involved was the first encounter with New South Wales at the Sydney Cricket Ground on 1 June 1946, before a huge crowd of 51,634.

New South Wales led 7–0 at half-time only to be beaten 14–10 after a match full of sensations. Among the incidents was Ike Owens's first British try and the questioning of referee Tom McMahon's decision by people situated in the Old Members' Stand. From there it seemed that Owens had knocked on before gathering the ball. People in other parts of the ground, however, saw that it was the New South Wales stand-off Pat Devery who had propelled the ball towards the New South Wales line.

New South Wales has shocking luck when Harry Bath, the outstanding forward in the interstate matches, was injured. He damaged a leg muscle and although he insisted on returning after half-time he was of little use to the side. This injury cost Bath probable selection for the test match.

When Bath was injured the scoring had not started and in fact there was no score for the first 30 minutes, then a dropped pass on the New South Wales '25' gave the home side a chance.

The brilliant Pat Devery snapped it up and sent Noel White sprinting along the touchline, Lisle had it next and then Bailey, with Clues backing up, was there to score between the posts. Jorgenson kicked the goal. A penalty by Jorgenson from four yards inside half-way gave New South Wales a 7–0 lead at the break.

Shortly after half-time Lisle was prominent twice; first he made a good run from the scrum base until stopped near the British line and then moved around the blind side of another scrum.

Devery, Jorgenson and Cooper handled in quick succession before Cooper dived over for the try; New South Wales were 10–0 ahead. The Lions stormed forward on attack. Their first points came after McCue had shot ahead from a scrum five yards out for Owens to score the disputed try. Risman missed the kick, but then reduced the New South Wales lead with a penalty from three yards inside the halfway line.

Prior to that New South Wales had been attacking with Hampstead and Cooper prominent, but a penalty gave Risman a chance from a difficult angle just outside the '25'. He goaled and New South Wales led 10–9.The tourists came again with Horne running hard before passing to Ward and on to Batten who went over in the corner. Ward converted and England had won 14–10.

The teams were:
New South Wales: J. Wedgwood (Dorrigo), L. Cooper (Easts), J. Jorgenson (Balmain – c), R .Bailey (Canterbury),N. White (Kurri), P. Devery (Balmain), S. Lisle (Easts), F. Farrell (Newtown), G. Watt (Easts), J. Munn (St George), A. Clues (Wests), H. Bath (Balmain), J. Hampstead (Balmain)

England: M. Ryan (Wigan), E. Batten (Bradford N), A.J. Risman (Salford – c), E. Ward (Bradford N), A. Johnson (Warrington), W. Horne (Barrow), T. McCue (Widnes), F. Whitcombe (Bradford N), J. Egan (Wigan), K. Gee (Wigan), L. White (York), T. Foster (Bradford N), I. Owens (Leeds)

The tourists then had a convincing 21–7 win over New South Wales in the second match at the Cricket Ground on 8 June in front of a crowd of 47,085. They had led 14–2 at half-time. Seven of the New South Wales team and 10 of the Lions played in the first test nine days later.

In this match Owens gave possibly his brightest display of the tour, he made the first two tries possible by clever anticipation backed up by the judgment expected from a class loose-forward.

New South Wales, down 2–0 early to a Jorgenson goal, were attacking and had reduced the leeway when Owens made the first English try. Gilbert had won a scrum for New South Wales on the English side of halfway and Lisle grubber-kicked the ball, which, moving at great speed, was trapped by Owens on his knees and when he gathered it properly he raced ahead, drawing the defence. He veered across field and then threw a pass to Jack Kitching who went straight down the field at top speed to score, Risman goaled and England led 9–2.

Soon after this, Wedgwood kicked to Ryan, who passed to Owens. He went across the field, and then kicked to the right wing, the ball bounced up for winger Bassett to gather it before Cooper could and go on to score, Risman goaled with a good kick and the Lions had a 14–2 half-time lead.

A high tackle knocked out Newham early in the second half but he returned to the game after a spell. Clues lost possession when he seemed certain to score, but finally Jorgenson goaled from outside the '25'.

A fine run by Egan earned a try which Risman converted for a 19–4 lead before handling by Australians Lisle, Bennett, Bailey and Jorgenson got the ball out to Cooper who gathered to score. Risman then kicked his sixth goal from a penalty to complete the scoring.

The teams were:

New South Wales: J. Wedgwood (Dorrigo), L. Cooper (Easts), J. Jorgenson (Balmain – c), R. Bailey (Canterbury),E. Newham (Cowra), E. Bennett (Wests), S. Lisle (Easts), A. Gibbs (South Newcastle), H. Gilbert (Balmain), F. Farrell (Newtown), S. Hobson (Easts), A.C. Clues (Wests), N. Mulligan (Newtown)

Great Britain: A.J. Risman (Salford – c), A. Johnson (Warrington), J. Kitching (Bradford N), E. Ward (Wigan), A. Bassett (Halifax), W. Davies (Bradford N), M. Ryan (Wigan), K Gee (Wigan), J. Egan (Wigan), F. Whitcombe (Bradford N), D. Phillips (Oldham), L. White (York), I. Owens (Leeds)

Cooper's meteoric rise saw him selected on the left wing for Australia in the first test against England at the Sydney Cricket Ground on 17 June 1946.The match ended 8–8; Australia missed an easy shot at goal close to the finish. Also in the Australian side were Pat Devery at stand-off, who later joined Hunter and Cooper at Huddersfield, and centre Ron Bailey who had previously played for Huddersfield.

The match provided some of the most remarkable scenes ever witnessed at any sporting fixture with police closing the gates as a safety measure with thousands still clamouring for admission at 11.30am. Even so, there was an official attendance of 64,527 with record takings of £10,130. Some fans had camped out all night to ensure a good seat, others arrived early and by 8am all the trams to the ground were packed. The New South Wales Rugby League realised that crowds would arrive early and staged a knockout competition, featuring the eight first grade Sydney teams, which started at 9am. The final was played after the test, which kicked off at 2pm. The Lions made one team change, Gus Risman played at full-back in place of Martin Ryan who had been injured in the match against Newcastle two days earlier.

Soon after the kick-off, the Lions harassed Australia on their goal-line, half-back Grice fumbled the ball; Horne pounced on it and dived over. Risman missed the conversion. Five minutes later Jorgenson landed a 35-yard penalty, which was his only success of the afternoon.

As to be expected, it was a spirited game. The only discordant note was the sending off of the English centre Jack Kitching in the 28th minute for punching Joe Jorgenson the Australian captain – after an alleged biting incident –and the game was handled with firmness by referee Tom McMahon. With half-time approaching England scored their second try, Ward short punted over the defence, cleverly regathered and sent big Frank Whitcombe in at the corner for an unconverted try.

Batten then made a great run racing down the touchline from his own '25' and as full-back Parkinson crouched low to make the tackle Batten suddenly took off and made a remarkable leap over Parkinson's head to go clear. However, Cooper, covering his full-back, caught him.

The Lions started the second half with Batten at centre in place of Kitching, with second-row Les White on the wing. The first few minutes saw Jorgenson and Risman fail with penalty kicks, but 11 minutes later hooker George Watt worked the ball to Bailey who scored with a splendid solo effort. With the Lions leading 6–5 with10 minutes left, Risman had a successful shot at goal as Farrell encroached offside.

Two of Australia's big successes had been full-back Dave Parkinson and Lionel Cooper, whose 70-yard try after 70 minutes saved the game for the home side. Trailing 8–5 and defending on their own '25' line, the ball went across the line to Bailey from a scrum, who in turn sent Cooper clear. He beat McCue at halfway and was into the English '25'. He veered inside Risman and swerved away for the try that levelled the scores. Jorgenson missed the conversion, and failed to land an easy 25-yard penalty three minutes later which could have given Australia a win.

It was a remarkable match for Cooper and Pat Devery to make their international debuts, although, because of the war, players on both sides had less experience than was the norm in an Ashes test.

Australia: D. Parkinson (Balmain), E. Newham (Cowra), J. Jorgenson (Balmain – c), R. Bailey (Canterbury), L.W. Cooper (Easts), P.C. Devery (Balmain), J. Grice (Souths, Brisbane), F. Farrell (Newtown), G. Watt (Easts), R. Westaway (Valleys, Brisbane), A.C. Clues (Wests), R. Kay (Souths, Brisbane), N.G. Mulligan (Newtown).
Scorers: Tries: Bailey, Cooper. Goal: Jorgenson.
England: A.J. Risman (Salford – c), E. Batten (Bradford N), E.Ward (Bradford N), J. Kitching (Bradford N), A.E. Johnson (Warrington), W. Horne (Barrow), T. McCue (Widnes), K. Gee (Wigan), J. Egan (Wigan), F.W. Whitcombe (Bradford N), L. White (York), D.V Phillips (Oldham), I.A. Owens (Leeds).
Scorers: Tries: Horne, Whitcombe. Goal: Risman.
Referee: T. McMahon (NSW)

The Lions won the second test at the Exhibition Ground in Brisbane on 6 July 1946, 14–5. They thus made sure of retaining the Ashes, and had dominated the clashes with Australia since the 1921–22 series.

Despite coal shortages, government-imposed travel restrictions and a public transport strike, the match created such an interest that officials closed the gates at 11.30am, three hours before the start. Although the official figures of 40,500 and takings of £5,190 were both records for Queensland, the exact attendance was never known as thousands broke into the ground before and after the gates were closed. The crowd flowed onto the playing area. Referee Stan Chambers had to clear them back before the first scrum went down.

The intensity level rose a notch or two from the first test – although the 'biting' incident was somewhat calmed when Canterbury's Ron Bailey replaced Jorgenson as Australia's captain. Both Lionel Cooper and Pat Devery kept their places in the team. This was a fierce match, with England's Joe Egan sent off just before the end when Ernest Ward was tackled by Arthur Clues, who seemed to throw a punch while Ward was on the ground. After the referee and linesman appeared not to do anything, an incensed Egan ran in and delivered Clues a perfect uppercut saying, "If the referee won't do his job, then someone has to".

Australia gave England too much latitude at the base of the scrum, with Hutchinson unable to handle Ike Owens who, along with Tommy McCue, dictated the game particularly round the scrum. Together they worked right wing moves, where Welsh winger Arthur Bassett's lethal finishing earned him a hat-trick of tries. Cooper, faced with the task of stopping Bassett, McCue and Owens did his best, but to no avail.

In a dour first half, Australia defended magnificently, but could not prevent the Lions from scoring twice. After 15 minutes McCue kicked through from a scrum just inside Australia's half, for Bassett to take the ball in his stride and cross in the corner. Ernest Ward missed the conversion, but kicked a touchline penalty six minutes before half-time.

Australia began the second half strongly, taking play to the English goalline where Gee was forced to concede a penalty. Jorgenson landed the goal, after which Bailey, from 40 yards out, ran and passed to Jorgenson who fed Cooper with four men in front of him and little room to move. However, he crashed through in typical style to score. Jorgenson missed the goal. Warrington's Albert Johnson then scored the try of the match five minutes from time. He chased a kick, juggled the ball on his fingertips above his head while running a full 15 yards, before he recovered it and went on to score in the corner. Australia again attacked with Watts and Westaway taking play to the English line, but Westaway was unable to release the ball when tackled. With three minutes left, Ted Ward raced downfield to put the match beyond doubt. He veered towards Bassett's wing, before passing to give him his third try.

Australia: D. Parkinson (Balmain), E. Newham (Cowra), R. Bailey (Canterbury – c), J. Jorgenson (Balmain), L.W. Cooper (Easts), P.C. Devery (Balmain), J. Grice (Souths, Brisbane), F. Farrell (Newtown), G. Watt (Easts), R. Westaway (Valleys, Brisbane), A.C. Clues (Wests), R. Kay (Souths, Brisbane), J. Hutchinson (Newcastle).

Scorers: Try: Cooper. Goal: Jorgensen.

England: E.Ward (Bradford N), A. Bassett (Halifax), A.J. Risman (Salford – c), E.H. Ward (Wigan), A.E. Johnson (Warrington), W. Horne (Barrow), T. McCue (Widnes), K. Gee (Wigan), J. Egan (Wigan), F.W. Whitcombe (Bradford N), L. White (York), D.V Phillips (Oldham), I.A. Owens (Leeds).

Scorers: Tries: Basset 3, Johnson. Goal: Ward.

Referee: S.W. Chambers (Queensland)

England won the third test 20–7 at the Sydney Cricket Ground on 20 July 1946. This meant that the visitors were the only Lions team to complete a three-match series in Australia undefeated. They won in front of a crowd of 35,294 with receipts of £4,572.

With the destination of the Ashes resolved, Australia took the opportunity to make changes. Ron Bailey, originally chosen as captain had to withdraw through injury, the captaincy reverting back to Joe Jorgenson. Edgar Newham was not selected.

In came Trevor Eather, the Boggabri centre and Kurri Kurri's Noel White who played on the wing. Clem Kennedy was preferred to Grice at scrum-half, with Jim Armstrong replacing Westaway at prop. Cooper and Devery kept their places.

Kennedy went on to give a great display, leaving the Australian selectors wondering just how valuable he would have been in the earlier tests when no one of similar ability was available. For England, George Curran, normally a hooker, replaced the unfit Frank Whitcombe at prop, and Eric Batten came in for Albert Johnson on the wing.

In a hard rugged game, in which it appeared several private scores needed settling from previous games during the tour, the game began disastrously for Australia with full-back Dave Parkinson suffering a broken leg after seven minutes – incredibly, with no substitutes allowed in those days, he courageously played on and had to be helped off the field at the end of the game.

The first half saw England squander many opportunities. Australia had to fight to take the chances that came their way. Cooper twice made timely interceptions. With the first he failed to score through weight of numbers and then was ankle-tapped by Risman when in the clear. Jorgenson landed a penalty goal for the Kangaroos after 17 minutes.

Owens and Bassett missed scoring chances by mishandling before Risman missed an easy penalty goal. He quickly atoned by dropping a goal from outside the Australian '25', which equalised the scores.

Things were looking up for the Aussies as Jorgenson kicked a further penalty goal, before Ernest Ward joined in a Lions attack, chipped the ball ahead, unfortunately into the arms of Clem Kennedy who reached halfway and kicked ahead for hooker George Watt to collect and return it to Kennedy who dived over for try to make it 7–2 at the break.

Six minutes following the interval, with the Lions in a different frame of mind, Risman landed a penalty goal, and with tries apiece from Bassett and Curran, posted an eight-point lead which they never relinquished.

Australia irretrievably lost the game in the 63rd minute when Arthur Clues struck out at Willie Horne in a tackle and was sent off, the game becoming decidedly scrappy.

Eric Batten, running from inside his own '25' almost to the Australian line, created a superb try for Ike Owens to touch down, Risman converting from under the posts as time ran out, but not before Gee fired out a long pass from a ruck to send in Bassett from 40 yards out, Ted Ward kicked the goal after the final whistle.

The game marked the end of Gus Risman's test career which had begun back in 1932, coincidentally on the same ground. Lionel Cooper had scored two tries, half of Australia's total.

The teams were:

Australia: D. Parkinson (Balmain), N. White (Kurri), J. Jorgenson (Balmain – c), T. Eather (Boggabri), L.W. Cooper (Easts), P.C. Devery (Balmain), C. Kennedy (Souths), F. Farrell (Newtown), G. Watt (Easts), J. Armstrong (Souths), A.C. Clues (Wests), R. Kay (Souths, Brisbane), N.G. Mulligan (Newtown)

Scorers: Try: Kennedy. Goals: Jorgensen 2.

England: E. Ward (Bradford N), A. Bassett (Halifax), A.J. Risman (Salford -c), E.H. Ward (Wigan), E. Batten (Bradford N), W. Horne (Barrow), T. McCue (Widnes), K. Gee (Wigan), J. Egan (Wigan), G. Curran (Salford), L. White (York), D.V Phillips (Oldham), I.A. Owens (Leeds).

Scorers: Tries: Bassett 2, Curran, Owens. Goals: Risman 3, E.H. Ward.

Referee: T. McMahon (NSW)

Both Lionel Cooper and Pat Devery emerged from the test series against England with great credit – Cooper voted as Australia's outstanding Player of the Year for 1946.

Interviewed for this book, Devery said that the test matches were a revelation to him, for it showed how much more professional the British side was and how much ground Australia needed to make up to compete with them – Australia had talent, but he felt lacked professionalism.

Pat Devery, who was rated as one of the major stars of the Australian side, also shone in the 1946 interstate series against Queensland, particularly in the final game which NSW won 30–14.

A review of the match quoted in Ray Chesterman's book *Tiger, Tiger, Burning Bright* said: "No better football has been seen this season than that played by Pat Devery who was hero of the match. The Balmain five-eighth was always dangerous in possession and when it came to defence, he was capable of holding his own with the best of them. Everything Devery did was class. His try, when he went on the blind side and had three tacklers fail to put a hand on him was one example."

His faultless handling, plus his ability to sidestep off either foot, did indeed stamp him out as a future star. It was Devery's first full season of senior rugby. After the 1947 season, when he captained New South

Wales to a 3–1 series win against Queensland, Devery joined Huddersfield.

Although Lionel Cooper – the eldest of five brothers – had made the decision to play his rugby in England, his siblings followed him into the Australian competition.

Cec Cooper joined Canterbury as a centre from junior club Lakemba, and progressed through the lower grades before making his first-grade debut against Newtown on 6 August 1949.In 1950, he secured a regular position which he maintained for the next four seasons and in 1951 played for New South Wales against France.

In 1951 and 1953, Cec captained the first-grade side, and after leaving the club in 1953 he returned to play his last season of first grade rugby in 1956.From 1949 to 1956 he played 79 games for Canterbury and scored 29 tries. In 1957, he coached the reserve-grade team and in 1958 and 1959 became coach of the first-grade side.

Col Cooper also joined Canterbury, and playing mainly reserve-grade rugby before he made his first-grade debut against Parramatta on 19 August 1950, when Frank Flynn was injured for the last two games of the season. Col played 48 games between 1950 and 1954, and scored 17 tries, mainly from the wing.

Noel, who at the time of writing lives in Port Macquarie, New South Wales, played two games for St George in 1953, and scored two tries, while Lionel's youngest brother Reg, another winger, joined Canterbury in 1954, then moved to St George in 1955 where he played one game on the wing before playing in the lower grades in 1956 and 1957.

He rejoined Canterbury in 1958 to secure a regular place in first grade rugby. He played 12 games and scored two tries. He made a further two first grade appearances in 1959, and scored one try. At the time of writing, Reg currently resides in Campbelltown, New South Wales.

Hunter and Cooper were met off the flying boat at Poole by Mr J. Wood-Beever and Mr A. Dews, members of the Huddersfield Football Committee, and arrived in West Yorkshire in late February 1947. It was one of the coldest winters in living memory. The country was only just starting to recover from the war, and rationing was still in place.

They were joining one of the sport's great clubs. Formed in 1875, Huddersfield were one of the founder members of the Northern Union. They had dominated the sport in the period leading up to the First World War, but had also been Champions twice in the late 1920s and won the

Hunter and Cooper arrive in Huddersfield. Members of the Huddersfield Rugby League football committee, Richard Lockwood (left) and Bill Cunningham, welcome Lionel Cooper and Johnny Hunter on 24 February 1947.

Challenge Cup in 1933, as well as having regular successes in the Yorkshire League and Yorkshire Cup. Their home ground, Fartown, was one of the sport's iconic venues.

Neither Hunter nor Cooper would ever forget their first game in England. It was against Hull KR, in the mud and cold at Craven Park on 15 March 1947. It was a bitter day, the ground was inches deep in mud, and the players became plastered in it. The cold benumbed them so that they could hardly feel their extremities.

Indeed, Daddy, the Rovers stand-off, left the field before the end, his legs so numb he could not stand up. The conditions were so bad that Hunter collapsed in the bath at the end of the game.

The result, a 0–0 draw, was one of the few scoreless matches that Huddersfield have played. Rovers adapted better to the conditions, kept the ball on the ground, and so gave Hunter plenty to do. The Australian was reliable, and turned defence into attack whenever he could. Was this a sign of things to come?

Not much was seen of Cooper – it was hardly a day on which a wingman could be expected to shine, but whenever he had the ball he looked dangerous. The Huddersfield team that day was:

Johnny Hunter, Jock Anderson, Alex Fiddes, Bernard Madden, Lionel Cooper, Russ Pepperell, W. Glyn Morgan, Bob Nicholson, Harold Whitehead, Des Thomas, Bob Robson, Les Baxter, Alex Givvons.

Surprisingly, Hunter looked a better prospect in their first few months at Huddersfield. Cooper took longer to settle down, although he did manage to score 10 tries in his first 12 matches.

Their first points for the Fartowners came in the same match, a 19–2 win against Bradford Northern at Odsal on 7 April 1947.Each player scored a try, and Cooper went on to register his first hat-trick of tries for Huddersfield in a 41–11 win over Hull KR in the last match of the season at Fartown on 26 May 1947. The season had been extended because of the bad winter. Huddersfield finished seventh in the league table with 50 points, just two points outside the top four clubs who contested the play-offs for the Championship.

In the July 1947 edition of *Rugby League Review*, A.N. Gaulton commented: "Huddersfield brought Cooper and Hunter over in February and are expecting great things from them next season. The same club has now secured the services of another Australian international in Pat Devery, a brilliant stand-off half and fine goalkicker."

Huddersfield made a decent start to the 1947–48 season, winning six and drawing two of their first eight games. Cooper was soon into his stride with a hat-trick of tries in the first leg of the first round of the Yorkshire Cup against Bramley on 17 September 1947. Huddersfield reached the semi-final of this traditionally hard-fought competition, before going down 18–15 to Wakefield Trinity at Belle Vue on 15 October.

The Fartown supporters were now starting to recognise the contributions of Hunter and Cooper to their team. The following tribute was paid to Hunter by an anonymous contributor to the *Huddersfield Examiner Letter Bag* in May 1947: "May I express a personal appreciation of the brilliant display given by Fartown's Australian full-back John Hunter against Batley. Rarely, or perhaps never, have I seen a player with such an evident enjoyment of the game, to say nothing of a display reminiscent of Gwyn Thomas at his best.

It is evident that the Fartown supporters have some treats in store in the coming season, and it is equally evident that with more such ornaments to adorn the game the Rugby League would benefit greatly."

Despite his early success, there were some anomalies in Hunter's play to be ironed out. A.N. Gaulton commented in Hunter's testimonial booklet *Johnny 1947–1955:* "One of his eccentricities was when he was about to change direction while running with the ball. You always knew when that was about to happen because he would whirl an arm violently as though it was an aeroplane propeller. After a few doses of concussion he learnt to temper his enthusiasm with discretion – without losing anything of the attractiveness of his play in doing so. The result was that Hunter became one of the greatest full-backs the game has known, and thousands flocked to watch him play."

Cooper was, as wingmen go, not very fast. He was a straight runner; rather than go round opponents, he went through them. He had a strong physique that made him difficult to hold, along with a powerful hand-off and intelligent change of pace, which were starting to pay dividends.

Sydney City versus Country, 4 May 1946. Back: A. Folwell (selector), J. Hampstead, J. Spencer, B. Ryan, A. Clues, L. Cooper, F. Farrell, A. Johnston (coach); front: C. Kennedy, G. Watt, T. Kirk, R. Bailey (c), J. Jorgenson, H. Bath, P. Devery; seated at front: B. Gray (selector).

New South Wales squad versus Queensland, 1946. Back: Edgar Newham, George Watt, Jim Armstrong, Arthur Clues; third row: Alf Gibbs, Lionel Cooper, A.W. O'Connor (selector), Frank Farrell, Jack Hutchinson; second row: Dave Parkinson, Bill Wylie, B. Gray (selector), Albert 'Rickety' Johnston (coach and selector), Sid Hobson, Trevor Eather; front: Sel Lisle, Pat Devery, L.H. Chambers (co-manager), Ron Bailey (c), J.L. Moses (co-manager), Joe Jorgenson, Noel White. (Courtesy David Middleton – League Information Services Ltd)

23

New South Wales versus England, 1 June 1946.
Back: A. Gibbs, L. Cooper, S. Hobson; second row: F. Farrell, J. Hampstead, J. Munn, E. Newham, A. Clues, G. Watt; front row: T. Eather, P. Devery, J. Jorgenson (c), A. Johnston (coach), H. Bath, R. Bailey, N. White; seated: J. Wedgwood, S. Lisle.

Australia versus England, first test 17 June 1946. Back: George Watt, Noel Mulligan, Edgar Newham, Frank Farrell, Lionel Cooper; middle: Reg Kay, Ray Westaway, Pat Devery, Dave Parkinson; front: Arthur Clues, Johnny Grice, Albert 'Rickety' Johnston (coach), Joe Jorgenson (c), Ron Bailey. (Courtesy Pat Devery)

24

Australia versus England, Second Test, 6 July 1946. Cooper scores Australia's try, with Dave Parkinson (No. 1), Joe Jorgenson (No. 3) and Pat Devery (No. 6) in support. (Courtesy Ian Heads)

Australia versus England, second test, 6 July 1946. Lionel Cooper (right) sizes up England loose forward Ike Owens. (Courtesy Ian Heads)

Lionel Cooper in action in a club match for Eastern Suburbs at the
Sydney Cricket Ground. (Courtesy Ian Heads)

Lionel Cooper - Australia's Player of the Year for 1946. Left winger in all three
tests against England and in every match played by New South Wales.

3. Devery comes to Fartown

Patrick Charles Devery was born on 9 August 1922 in Tweed Heads on the North coast of New South Wales. After attending Tweed Heads Public School where he first played rugby league at the age of seven, he went to the nearest high school, Murwillumbah. He graduated and went to Armidale Teachers College in 1940, where he played scrum-half and centre. His first teaching assignment was to a one-teacher school with 25 students spanning grades 1 to 6 – the school was located in wheat country in western New South Wales.

Devery already had a good reputation, and scored seven tries on his debut for Fortitude Valley in the Brisbane League. Within six months he was conscripted into the Australian Army and began training to become an instructor; he later transferred to the Australian Navy.

It was while training as a radar operator in Sydney that he turned up at the Balmain club and asked for a trial. The club arranged to watch him in a third-grade game at Huntsville Oval, but because he had to use public transport, he missed the kick-off.

The next week he did play, which resulted in a quick rise to the reserve grade and then first grade. He scored two tries on his debut in a game against Souths at Leichardt Oval on 22 July 1944.

He was unable to play many matches because of his naval duties over the next couple of years, but he did play in Balmain's Grand Final against Newtown on 16 September 1944 at the Sydney Cricket Ground.

Newtown looked set for back-to-back titles after finishing as minor premiers. Balmain arrived in the finals in second place, one point behind Newtown. In their semi-finals, Newtown blitzed St George 55–7, and Balmain beat South Sydney 15–6.

Balmain met Newtown in the Final, and won a close game 19–16, which enabled Newtown to exercise their 'right of challenge', and they called for a Grand Final. In a low-scoring affair, Balmain's Joe Jorgenson kicked two late penalty goals to give the Tigers a 12–8 win and their eighth title. Devery and Keith Parkinson scored the tries. The teams were:

Balmain: Dave Parkinson, Arthur Patton (c), Joe Jorgenson, Tom Bourke, Keith Parkinson, Stan Ponchard, Pat Devery, Jack Hampstead, George Watt, Colin Campbell, Athol Smith, Sid Ryan, Dawson Buckley.
Scorers: Tries: Parkinson, Devery. Goals: Jorgensen 3.
Newtown: Tom Kirk, Sid Goodwin, Lin McClean, Bruce Ryan, Norm Jackson, Tom Nevin, Jack Kadwell, Charlie Montgomery, Jimmy Brailey, Frank Farrell (c),Keith Phillips, Len Ryan, Charles Cahill.
Scorers: Tries: McClean, Farrell. Goal: Kirk.

The 1945 season saw fourth-placed Balmain reach the final. However, they were beaten 22–18 by Easts, who included Hunter and Cooper. In1946, Balmain's Grand Final side had to fight hard in a close-fought contest to overcome St George 13–12 at the Sydney Sports Ground on 14 September. This was the club's ninth first grade premiership.

With just two rounds remaining, Newtown had looked on track for the minor premiership until they lost to Eastern Suburbs and then Balmain in the two final rounds of the year. This left St George to take the minor premiership, and with it a guaranteed place in the Final.

In spite of St George's status as minor premiers, Balmain were Grand Final favourites because of their comprehensive routing of the Dragons in the first semi-final.

A series of dubious decisions by referee George Bishop gave Balmain an advantage. There was a disallowed try by St George and two Balmain tries which came off what appeared to be forward passes, one when Balmain's Joe Jorgenson scored after receiving a ball that seemed to have been propelled at least a yard forward.

The Dragons came close to victory late in the game when Jack Lindwall scored in the corner but his brother Ray was unable to convert. He missed all four conversion attempts on the day.

The Tigers had won seven straight victories to take the premiership.
Balmain: Jack McCullough, Arthur Patton, Pat Devery, Tom Bourke (c), Joe Jorgenson, George Williams, Stan Ponchard, Hilton Kidd, Herb Gilbert Jnr, Jack Spencer, Fred de Belin, Harry Bath, Jack Hampstead.
Scorers: Tries: Jorgenson 2, Patton. Goals: Bourke 2.
St George: Ray Lindwall, Noel Jones, Doug McRitchie, Fred Brown, Jack Lindwall, Don Graham, Max Hayward, Jack Munn, Ken Banks, Jack McPherson, Jim Hale, Herb Narvo (c), Chick Donnelly.
Scorers: Tries: Jack Lindwall 2, Jones, Munn.

Success by Balmain, one of the original foundation clubs from 1908, capped an excellent record over the previous three seasons: winners in 1944, runners-up to Easts in 1945, and winners in 1946, a feat bettered only by the club's 1915 to 1917 run of successes.

Balmain, who had to battle hard for their victories, had also won the premiership in 1939.For all this success, much credit was attributable to club secretary Harold Matthews and his fellow officials who sought out the best players available for positions in which the club was weak without affecting the chances of younger players aiming to reach the top grade. In the 1946 Grand Final, Balmain fielded seven local products in Jack McCullough, Tommy Burke, who led the side, George Williams, Stan

Ponchard, Jack Hampstead, Hilton Kidd and Fred de Bellin. Pat Devery also learnt most of his football with Balmain.

Balmain's nine premierships equalled the record of Eastern Suburbs and was exceeded only by South Sydney's 11. In 1946, Balmain supplied more representative players than any other club. Joe Jorgenson captained Australia in the first and third tests and played in the second; Pat Devery and Jack Hampstead also featured in all three tests. This trio, along with Jack Hampstead, Harry Bath and Herb Gilbert also wore the light blue of New South Wales.

The Tigers strung together seven consecutive wins including a preliminary final victory over minor premiers Canterbury in their attempt at a second straight premiership. Canterbury exercised their 'right of challenge' after losing the final and called for a Grand Final decider on 20 September at the Sydney Sports Ground.

Balmain's Kangaroo captain Joe Jorgenson had played and coached on a country contract in Junee in 1947, but returned to the Tigers reserve-grade in time for the semi-finals. The Grand Final was his sole first-grade appearance of the season. Pat Devery was Balmain's nominated goalkicker, but after several misses he passed the duty over to Jorgenson who kicked three penalties to keep Balmain in the game, trailing 9–6 with just 10 minutes to go. Then Jorgenson crashed over for a try under the posts and after receiving medical attention converted to give the Tigers an 11–9 lead. A final penalty goal then sealed the match for the Tigers 13–9. Jorgenson was chaired from the field.

Canterbury-Bankstown: Richard Johnson, Jeff Simmonds, Eddie Tracy, Norm Young, Morrie Murphy, Ray Hasson, Bruce Hopkins, Eddie Burns, Roy Kirkaldy, Henry Porter (c), Alister Clarke, Ken Charlton, Len Holmes.
Scorers: Try: Hasson. Goals: Johnson 2, Hasson
Balmain: Jack McCullough, Robert Lulham, Pat Devery, Joe Jorgenson, Arthur Patton, George Williams, Des Bryan, Jack Branighan, Herb Gilbert Jnr, Jack Spencer, Sid Ryan, Harry Bath, Tom Bourke (c).
Scorer: Try: Jorgensen. Goals: Jorgensen 5.

Overall, Devery played 38 games for Balmain from 1944 to 1947; he scored 25 tries and kicked 59 goals. On 30 September 1947, Pat Devery arrived in England to play for Huddersfield. He just beat the renewal of the transfer ban.

Tweed Heads Public School Primary Class 1936. Back row: Pat Devery, Lloyd Taylor, Vince Soorley, Keith Harley, Kevin Faux; middle row: Arch Barton, Jim Shackley, Allan Bartley, Lyle Bailey, Gordon Birkett, Ian Petherick, Jack Newell; front row: Beryl Neden, Grace Gillette, May Eadie, Coral Armstrong, Norma Townsend. The headmaster was Albert Williams. (Courtesy Pat Devery).

Balmain – First Grade Premiers, 1946. Back: A. Toby, C. Richards, T. Prescott, D. Cooksey, H. Matthews, N. Robinson, L. Lee; second row: P. Devery, J. Jorgenson, M. Kidd, A. Patton, J. Hampstead, J. Spencer, H. Gilbert, F. de Belin; seated: K. Parkinson, S. Ryan, G. Williams, T. Bourke, H. Bath, D. Parkinson, R. Paterson; front (on ground): J. McCullough, F. Porter (ball boy), S. Ponchard. (Courtesy Ian Heads)

Pat Devery played at stand-off in all three tests for Australia against England in 1946.
(Courtesy Pat Devery)

Pat Devery and Harry Bath bid farewell to Balmain. After Balmain had beaten Canterbury in the 1947 Grand Final, Pat Devery (seated, left) and Harry Bath headed to England to play club rugby league. (Courtesy Ian Heads)

Rugby League Parade, winter 1947–48, featuring 'Australians on Parade', with Harry Bath and Pat Devery on the front cover.

Huddersfield rugby league team 1947–48. Back: John Maiden, Lionel Cooper, Dave Valentine, Bob Robson, Harold Whitehead, Des Thomas; middle: Harold Holt (assistant trainer), Johnny Hunter, Russ Pepperell, Pat Devery (c), Jock Anderson, Jeff Bawden, Alex Fiddes (trainer); front: Paddy Walsh, Bob Nicholson.

The news in the Australian press that Devery had accepted an offer of a three-year contract for £1,300, plus match pay and an assured job in his profession as a teacher, was a bombshell to rugby league enthusiasts down under. He had good company on the journey; with him on the plane were Harry Bath and Len Kenny, who were bound for Barrow and Leeds respectively. Bath had missed the test series through injury, and because the Australians did not select players who were playing overseas, never played for his country. Alan Whiticker and Ian Collis say that he would have been certain to win this honour, but then went to England when "with the lifting of the international poaching bans, the wealthy English clubs plundered the best players Australia had to offer." [3]

Devery was met at Poole Airport by Bill Cunningham on behalf of the club, and immediately travelled north. He made his debut for Huddersfield at stand-off against Workington Town at Derwent Park on 4 October 1947. He made a good impression though he was plainly finding his feet with his new team-mates.

Workington kicked off and after a desultory kicking exchange between Gus Risman and Hunter, Albert Pepperell set the crowd alight with a clever run half the length of the field.

Devery came into the picture with a tackle on Risman that put Huddersfield on the home '25' but, when the Fartowners were penalised, Risman found touch near the line. Huddersfield then set up an attack, and Cooper made half the length of the field with a strong run.

It was nip and tuck with neither side able to break down the other, but from a scrum near the Fartown line, Gibson, Risman and Jackson swept up field in a movement that saw Jackson score a try. Risman converted to make the half-time score 5–0 to Workington.

Devery came more into the game and worked a move with Morgan that put Huddersfield on the attack after the interval, but the Fartowners were their own worst enemy and lost ground through handling errors.

Workington replied with a passing move that promised another try, but Cooper intercepted, and with the help of Russ Pepperell and Hunter ran the ball to the home '25'.

Hunter was stopped when he seemed to be through, but was hurt in doing so and had to be taken off with a head injury. Russ Pepperell took his place at full-back until his return a few minutes later, however, Hunter was far from well and had to go off again.

Workington began to put pressure on Huddersfield and, when the Fartowners were penalised on their own '25', Risman kicked a goal.

---

[3] *Rugby League test matches in Australia* by Alan Whiticker and Ian Collis, p.79

Workington attacked again and Risman put in a kick that bounced nicely for him, ran to halfway before throwing out a long pass to Park who scored wide out. Risman missed the conversion. Workington's Ivison was then sent off for tripping and Huddersfield staged a late rally. Cooper went over in the corner, but Jeff Bawden missed the kick.

Workington Town: Risman, McGilvary, Rogers, Jackson, Jepson, Gibson, A. Pepperell, Hodson, Ackerley, Hayton, Park, Wareing, Ivison.

Huddersfield: Johnny Hunter, Russ Pepperell, Bernard Madden, Jeff Bawden, Lionel Cooper, Pat Devery, W. Glyn Morgan, Tom Taylor, Harold Whitehead, Bob Nicholson, Les Baxter, Des Thomas, Alex Givvons.

The following week, on 11 October, Devery made his home debut against Castleford in a 50–5 win at Fartown. He delighted the 13,000 crowd, and played a big part in three of the four tries Huddersfield scored in the first half. Castleford opened the scoring. Morgan, trying to clear his own line, had his kick charged down by Lewis who touched down for a try, Staines kicked the goal.

The scores were levelled when Devery came into the picture with a beautiful run through the middle. He passed to Bawden who in turn fed Madden who went over near the posts, Bawden kicked the goal.

Huddersfield now had the upper hand and were soon in the lead when Morgan put in a short kick for Bawden to follow, steering the ball over the line to score, Devery missed the kick at goal.

Huddersfield kept up the attack, with Cooper and Oughton prominent. Devery then made another neat burst up the middle and passed out to Nicholson to finish with a try; but Bawden was unable to convert.

The fourth try came largely through Devery. The Australian beat one man and opened out play with a pass to Bawden. He in turn fed Cooper to score in the corner, which made the half-time score 14–5 to Huddersfield.

The second half was only two minutes old when good work by Givvons and Morgan led to Baxter scoring. Devery kicked his first points for the club. Cooper and Bawden then combined with some close passing to put Oughton in at the corner. Devery added the goal points with a fine kick. Moments later he was wide with a penalty kick at goal, but after a 30 yard run, Cooper forced his way over in the corner. Devery landed a superb touchline conversion.

Devery was everywhere, and cut through once again to put Cooper in for the eighth Huddersfield try; however, the kick was unsuccessful. A beautiful break, again by Devery, put Huddersfield on the visitors' line and from the subsequent play-the-ball Nicholson went over under the posts. Devery converted. After a 50-yard run up field, Pepperell gave the ball to Nicholson who finished the remainder of the distance to score his third try by the posts. Devery converted again.

The next try was Devery's – a beautiful solo effort – the stand-off ran the ball 50 yards to score, and added the conversion for good measure. A try by Cooper after a run half the length of the field brought up the 50 points for the Fartowners. Devery, who scored a try and kicked six goals for a total of 15 points, had certainly made his mark.

Another significant arrival at Fartown was that of David Donald Valentine from Hawick RUFC in the Scottish Borders. Football committee chairman Bill Cunningham, himself also a Scot, persuaded him to sign professional forms on 11 October 1947.

Devery played stand-off in his first eight games for Huddersfield, before he moved to left centre in a 12–7 win against the New Zealanders at Fartown on 22 November 1947. The Kiwis fielded10 test players.

At the turn of the year, Huddersfield were still undefeated at home. Cooper continued his scoring streak with another four-try haul in a 34–0 defeat of Bramley at Barley Mow on 10 January 1948. Jock Anderson matched him with four tries of his own. Consistently scoring throughout the season, Cooper scored a further hat-trick at Fartown against York on 20 March. Devery also helped himself to a treble at Post Office Road against Featherstone Rovers in a 29–3 win on 29 March.

But for the third successive season, no cups found their way to Fartown. Many times during the season the team raised high hopes among their followers, only to dash them to the ground with displays for which there were no excuses. In the Challenge Cup, after beating the holders Bradford Northern 6–2 at Fartown in the first round, first leg, Huddersfield went down 15–2 at Odsal to go out 17–8 on aggregate. In the Yorkshire Cup, after dispatching Bramley and Keighley, the Fartowners lost 18–15 at Belle Vue to Wakefield Trinity in the semi-final.

Their final display, in the Championship semi-final at Wilderspool – a 17–5 loss to Warrington – was the crowning disappointment. However, there was some improvement compared to 1946–47, when they had finished seventh in the league. This time Huddersfield were third and runners-up in the Yorkshire League. Cooper finished with 37 tries for the season, and was third in the national try scorers list. Fellow Australian Brian Bevan led the list with 57.

Hopes were high at Fartown as the 1948–49 season beckoned. Pat Devery was reappointed as captain and the team had been strengthened in the close season with the signing of John Christopher Daly, an Irish rugby union international front-row forward and Welshman William Martin (Billy) Banks, a scrum-half from Wakefield Trinity, for £1,850.

"Autolycus" in the *Huddersfield Examiner* looked at the coming season with a great deal of optimism and said: "Huddersfield have this year the promise of being a Championship side...the Australians, I feel, are likely to do better this season now that they are fully acclimatised. That I think is very true of Devery, who came to Huddersfield after a full season 'down under' and showed a little staleness towards the end. I don't think we have seen the best of Devery yet...Cooper is likely to prove a prolific try-scorer again; he is a wing of a totally different type. He doesn't need much room to get going, and once he is off he takes some stopping.

Hunter will improve if he disciplines his enthusiasm. His brilliance is not to be denied...he takes chances that involve risks, but experience will teach him to sort thing out, and without doubt make him the best full-back in the league."

In those days professional rugby league was part-time. Lionel Cooper worked as rep for Fina Petroleum, while Hunter was employed for some time as a plumber working for Harry Littlewood at Fartown, also later as a carpet salesman. Pat Devery worked as a teacher

Diana Beaumont Armitage (neé Heppenstall) in an email to the author recalled that: "My father, Harry Heppenstall, was a great rugby league fan, and when the chairman of Huddersfield asked him to find a job for an Australian [Hunter] he did. My grandparents were Mr and Mrs Norman Heppenstall and they owned and ran a company called Beaumont's Warehouse in Imperial Yard off New Street, Huddersfield, where all the family worked. Not only did we employ Johnny as a salesman in the carpet department, but he was a lodger at our house in Shelley Woodhouse for years... We at Beaumont's liked Johnny, Dave Valentine was also our joiner, and his wife Effie worked in our order department..."

4. Champions

How good really was this Huddersfield side? After a workmanlike 23–5 win at Featherstone on the first day of the season, 21 August 1948, that question was answered the following week when cup-holders Wigan came to Fartown for the first home game of the season.

Huddersfield humbled Wigan 24–5 – Wigan's heaviest defeat since the War – in front of a crowd of 24,589, in what was one of the best displays seen at Fartown for many a year.

Hunter, Walsh, Valentine and Cooper scored tries and Bawden kicked six goals. White scored Wigan's try and Ward kicked a goal. Hunter was in great form, more often than not an extra threequarter than a full-back, but was never caught out of position.

The *Rugby League Review's* report of the match said: "In view of the Huddersfield team work, to select a man-of-the-match from a side in which all shone is no easy task, but we think the honour should go to Hunter, the Huddersfield full-back. Hunter is more than a footballer – he is an entertainment! His flying dives, his eye for the opening that turns defence into attack, and his capacity for bobbing up from nowhere. He is one of the personalities of the game." The writer continued: "Ratcliffe, like many another wing before him, found the lively Cooper a handful."

Yorkshire County Amateurs provided the opposition at Fartown on 11 September in the first leg of the first round of the Yorkshire Cup – to bring a representative amateur side into the competition may have helped the junior section of the code, but hardly, except from a financial aspect, when the draw paired them against opponents as strong as Huddersfield. Cooper alone was far too much of a handful for the amateurs and had a field day scoring eight tries in a 79–5 trouncing.

In the second leg at Dewsbury a week later, Cooper scored seven tries as the amateurs capitulated 61–0, 140–5 on aggregate, and the Fartowners progressed to the second round. However, Bradford Northern, who had already lost three of their six league games, beat them 19–12 on 20 September at Odsal to knock them out of the competition. This game was just two days after Huddersfield had played a bruising encounter with the 1948 Australian tourists at Fartown.

For the tour's opening match, 26,053 turned out to watch a game full of thrills and incident which had the Huddersfield supporters baying for Australian blood due to a number of off-the-ball clashes – any doubts about the tour opening with a tame exhibition match were soon dispelled.

The tourists fully held their own in a first half of good lively rugby – they were only 2–0 down to a Bawden penalty goal. However, with the game gradually slipping out of the Australians' grasp and with the tourists looking leg weary, Reid and Robson scored two tries each for Huddersfield. Devery, with three, and Bawden added the goals. O'Connell scored Australia's try; the final score of 22–3 sealed a great afternoon for the Fartowners.

In the second half Hunter was felled and rendered unconscious from a high shot from winger John 'Whacka' Graves who only received a lecture from referee Stan Adams. Hunter was carried off on a stretcher and the crowd called for Graves's blood.

At the end of the game, the crowd climbed over the railings and headed for Graves, but Arthur Archbell, Huddersfield's secretary reacted quickly and ordered the Duke of Wellington's West Riding Regimental band to strike up *God save the King.* The patriotic crowd stood to attention while Graves headed quickly to the dressing room! The ill feeling continued after the game, when one Huddersfield club official was heard to call the Australians the "filthiest team ever sent to Great Britain's shores." [4]

It was a tough opening to the tour for the Kangaroos. Ian Heads outlines that "...Fred de Belin... suffered a spiral fracture of the right leg... Bill Tyquin chipped an elbow and winger Johnny Graves badly sprained an ankle." [5] The teams that day were:

Huddersfield: Johnny Hunter, Russ Pepperell, Jeff Bawden, Paddy Reid, Lionel Cooper, Pat Devery, Stan Walsh, John Maiden, Mel Meek, John Daly, Bob Robson, Bob Nicholson, Dave Valentine.
Australia: Clive Churchill, Pat McMahon, Col Maxwell, Len Pegg, Johnny Graves, Wally O'Connell, Keith Froome, Jack Holland, Kevin Schubert, Alf Gibbs, Duncan Hall, Fred de Belin, Bill Tyquin.

Cooper was in good try-scoring form. He notched four in a 35–8 win against Workington Town at Fartown on 16 October, and managed hat-tricks against Hull KR at Craven Park on 16 November, when he reached 100 points for the season, and at Fartown against Halifax in a 32–3 Boxing Day win. He headed the try scorers with 41 at the turn of the season, 10 more than Brian Bevan, his great rival at Warrington.

In December 1948, Pat Devery moved to centre, after the club signed Archie Ferguson, a Scottish stand-off. *Rugby League Review*

---

[4] Quoted in *The Kangaroos* by Ian Heads, p.113
[5] *The Kangaroos* by Ian Heads, p.112

commented: "Many Fartowners prefer to see Devery at centre and have great hopes of this all-Australian left wing." It added: "Hunter, that most venturesome of all full-backs, has been handicapped by injury."

Huddersfield, then in fourth place in the table, were clearly leaving no stone unturned in the quest for honours, and signed the Castleford and former test loose-forward Ike Owens for a fee of £2,750 on 19 January 1949. It was the biggest transfer fee Huddersfield had paid for a forward.

In the Challenge Cup, Huddersfield reached the semi-final, on the way overcoming Rochdale Hornets 15–5 on aggregate in a two-legged affair in the first round, Workington Town 3–0 at Fartown, and Leeds in the quarter-final at Headingley 20–9. Leeds played most of the game with 12 men after front-row forward Gwyn Gronow was dismissed for an alleged trip on Cooper.

The week before the semi-final, Huddersfield beat Hunslet 15–9at Parkside. *Rugby League Review* commented: "For the man-of-the-match … I select Pat Devery, who played a real captain's part. Devery can make the game look easy and always appears to be playing well within himself. His try on this occasion was a lovely piece of work and must have amazed the two Hunslet defenders who seemed to have him well covered."

The semi-final was against local rivals Halifax at Odsal Stadium on 2 April before a crowd of 64,250. *Rugby League Review*'s preview highlighted the role of the team's Australian stars: "The Huddersfield 'stars' will certainly scintillate at Odsal. First, the three Australians – popular Johnny Hunter, grand and oft-times spectacular full-back; Lionel Cooper, the finest winger in the game today, and Pat Devery, captain and strategist with few equals."

However, Halifax dramatically beat Huddersfield 11–10. The Fartowners were 10–2 up at the interval. When the sides changed ends no-one in either camp could have doubted Huddersfield were on top, but one slip 10 minutes from time ended their cup hopes. A mix up between Ferguson, who was playing full-back for the first time instead of Hunter, who missed the match through injury, and Pepperell allowing Kielty to touchdown.

Ironically, after the shock defeat to Halifax, the culmination of a great run of nine straight league wins, scoring more than 200 points, ensured third place in the league table, which meant a trip to Wigan in the Championship semi-final on 30 April.

Huddersfield, who were presented with the Yorkshire League trophy before the game, began well before an all-ticket record crowd of 42,700 at Central Park.

Bawden opened the scoring for Huddersfield with a penalty, but the Fartowners fell away after 20 minutes when poor handling in front of their own posts gave Wigan a penalty they promptly accepted. Ward kicked the goal. He then scored an unconverted try to put Wigan 5–2 ahead at the break.

Wigan's interval lead was wiped out by a Cooper try and, with nine points in the last 15minutes; Huddersfield won 14–5, to secure the right to meet Warrington in the League Championship Final at Maine Road, Manchester, on 14 May 1949.

There was behind-the-scenes drama before the game started. Frank Smith, the appointed referee, did not receive the official notification of his appointment and did not travel to Maine Road. It later transpired that the document had been lost in the post. His place was taken by one of the touch judges, Matt Coates of Pudsey, and Paul Cowell, a referee who was attending the match as a spectator ran the line in Coates's place.

The first half was one of brilliant play in which Huddersfield built up an eight-point lead. Warrington kicked off, but Huddersfield were in their stride almost immediately, the ball moved out to Cooper, but the wingman was not allowed to go far by the Warrington defence.

A penalty put Huddersfield over their opponents' 25 yard line, but Warrington heeled the ball from the next couple of scrums to clear their line. Huddersfield regained possession, Cooper picked up a loose ball, ran through, kicked ahead and caught the ball as it bounced only to be stopped two yards from the line.

This put the Fartowners in a strong position and a try seemed likely when the ball came across to Devery, but Cooper failed to hold the final pass and the chance was gone. A brilliant run by Ferguson and kick by Hunter which found touch near the corner flag helped Huddersfield keep up the pressure.

Warrington worked their way back up the field. It was the first time in 10 minutes that they had been in the Huddersfield half. Their stay was a brief one because Anderson broke away for the Fartowners on the right, kicked and regathered. The ball went loose after being fumbled by a Warrington defender and Valentine regained possession to give Daly a try between the posts. Devery converted.

The game gained fresh impetuous as Warrington swept back on the attack and opened out the play to Bevan who was pushed into touch 10 yards from the Fartowners' line. The Warrington forwards tried short rushes, but the Huddersfield pack tackled superbly and gradually gained ground through passing moves.

A kick to touch put Warrington back on the Huddersfield '25', Helme and Fleming worked a reverse pass cleverly, with Fleming all but clear before Hunter brought him down with a great cover tackle.

A burst by Devery and kick by Bevan kept the game going at a lively pace, and excitement rose as Bevan got away again only for Valentine to stop him in his tracks. Half-time beckoned as a Huddersfield move almost went the length of the field. Banks and Devery combined smartly before Devery received the ball for a second time and passed to Cooper, who went in at the corner. It was too far out for Devery to kick the goal.

A run and kick from Hunter drove back another Warrington attack, but a run and kick-through by Bevan who saw the ball run dead in goal ended a brilliant first half with Huddersfield 8–0 to the good. Warrington began the second half by monopolising possession from the first five scrums before Anderson got his boot to a dropped pass and forced them back to halfway. A 40-yard run by Cooper got Huddersfield back on the attack, but Jones regained a lot of ground with a neat touch-finding kick.

Huddersfield went further in front when Anderson dribbled the ball forward and Devery came up at speed to snap up the rolling ball to score under the posts. He added the two extra points.

Warrington were not done by any means and were awarded two penalties inside the Huddersfield half; from the second Palin kicked a goal. The Wire continued to carry the attack to Huddersfield, and their sustained pressure was rewarded when Francis scored a try in the corner a few minutes from the end; Bath kicked a superb touchline goal.

Things were tense and almost immediately Jackson scored for Warrington; Bath converted. Huddersfield held on grimly to win 13–12.

Devery had a fine game, his smother tackles on Pimblett gave the Warrington backs little room in which to move. Vincent Firth, in *Rugby League Review,* picked out Devery as his man-of-the-match. He commented: "The Fartowners owed most of their success to the matchless generalship of the captain Pat Devery. His was the guiding hand that piloted his side to victory. Even in the first half his patience and skill in getting the team underway was very obvious, while the second half showed Devery for what he is, one of the finest, aye the finest centre threequarter in rugby league football today."

Hunter put in one of his best displays in a Fartown jersey, and managed time after time to turn defence into attack.

It was Huddersfield's sixth championship. The club's previous successes were in 1912, 1913, 1915, 1929 and 1930.

The attendance was 75,194 – the best at that time for any rugby league game in England apart from those at Wembley. However, the ground was very full, and some supporters complained that they could not see the game.

Huddersfield: J.C.H. Hunter, J. Anderson, A. Ferguson, P.C. Devery, L.W. Cooper, G.R. Pepperell, W.M. Banks, M.J. Maiden, A.M. Meek, J.C. Daly, I.A. Owens, R. Nicholson, D.D. Valentine.
Scorers: Tries: Devery, Cooper, Daly. Goals: Devery 2.
Warrington: L. Jones, B. Bevan, A.J. Pimblett, W. Jackson, R.L. Francis, G.J. Helme, W. Derbyshire, H.H. Fishwick, W. Riley, A.H. Bath, J.J. Featherstone, H. Palin.
Scorers: Tries: Jackson, Francis. Goals: Bath 2, Palin.
Referee: Matt Coates (Pudsey)

It had been Huddersfield's most successful season for 19 years. Cooper had improved and scored 60 tries to head the national try-scorers list, four clear of Brian Bevan. In the club's history, his total for a season was bettered only by Rosenfeld's 80 in 1913–14. Devery contributed 20 tries and kicked 40 goals; Jeff Bawden finished the season with 103 goals.

A. N. Gaulton said in *Rugby League Review* that "In classing Devery's team with that led by the immortal 'Waggy', the Fartown old-timers have paid their present side the highest possible compliment."

Huddersfield 49 Featherstone Rovers 7 at Fartown, 19 April 1949.
Lionel Cooper beats the defence to score behind the posts, and finished the game with a hat-trick of tries. Hunter also scored three tries.
(Courtesy *Huddersfield Examiner*)

Huddersfield 13 Warrington 12, Championship Final at Maine Road on 14 May 1949. Pat Devery scoring Huddersfield's third try after a 50 yard run, Ferguson backing up, with Anderson and Nicholson (right) in the background.

Huddersfield rugby league team 1948–49: winners of the Championship and Yorkshire League. Back: S. Williams, H. Lockwood, B. Gronow, W. Cunningham (chairman), H.V. Wood(president), J. Wood-Beever (vice-chairman), A. Dews, W. Stoker; third row: R. Nicholson, J. Maiden, J.C. Daly, R.S. Robson, D.D. Valentine, J.L. Davies, I.A. Owens, G.V. Hughes; seated: A. Archbell (secretary), G. Wilson, J. Anderson, J. Bawden, P.C. Devery (c), L.W. Cooper, J.C.H. Hunter, M. Meek, A.E. Fiddes (trainer); front: S.V. Pepperell, W. Banks, G.R. Pepperell, A. Ferguson.

Pat Devery, the Huddersfield captain, holds the Championship trophy after beating Warrington 13–12 at Maine Road.

Huddersfield 27 Hunslet 10 at Fartown, 8 October 1949.
Lionel Cooper held in the tackle, with Fartowners Maiden, Valentine
and Pritchard looking on. (Courtesy *Huddersfield Examiner*)

The Huddersfield rugby league team at Huddersfield Town Hall.
Pat Devery holding the Championship trophy, Jeff Bawden holding the Yorkshire
League trophy after Huddersfield had beaten Warrington in the 1949
Championship Final. (Courtesy *Huddersfield Examiner*)

Huddersfield rugby league team 1949–50 – Championship and Yorkshire Cup
beaten finalists. Back: Dick Cracknell, Jim Bowden, Ike Owens, Bob Nicholson,
Frank Wagstaff, Dave Valentine; seated: Arthur Wilmot, Lionel Cooper, Pat
Devery (c), Johnny Hunter, Mel Meek; front: Billy Banks, Russ Pepperell.

45

Huddersfield ended 1948–49 as champions and there was no reason to believe that 1949–50 should be any worse. A.N. Gaulton commented in *Rugby League Review* that the team could be seen as a one-man side with Cooper scoring so many tries, but continued: "True enough, Cooper was looked upon as the danger point by opponents, but Lionel himself is the first to express his acknowledgements to his colleagues who paved the way for so many of his tries. Even Hunter ran in 16 tries from full-back, which must surely be a league record... Devery, too, was frequently among the scorers with both tries and goals."

The Fartowners began the new season with five straight victories. On 3 September, Huddersfield beat Warrington 25–17 at Fartown, which allowed a comparison between the two great Australian wingers.

D' Artagnan (A.N. Gaulton) wrote in *Rugby League Review*: "It was interesting to watch the contrasting styles of these two Australians. Bevan, with is long striding wide step, darting here and there, and Cooper matching this with straight, forceful running and his powerful hand-off."

The winning run ended at Salford on 7 September. The team's hopes of a good run in the Yorkshire Cup began positively with a first round 29–13 aggregate win over Leeds, and a 20–12 win over Wakefield Trinity in the second round at Fartown.

Cooper was being recognised as a great threat. Vincent Firth wrote in *Rugby League Review*: "The business of successfully tackling Cooper, the Fartown winger, becomes more and more of a problem to opposing sides. Leeds more or less solved the problem, by deputing three of their men to keep the Australian in check."

In a 22–12 defeat at Wigan, he scored both tries for the Fartowners. Firth wrote: "... from the ensuing scrum Cooper got possession and scored one of his rip-roaring tries, giving three opponents each a perfect example of his faultless hand-off." He continued: "...Cooper [scored] another beautiful try, which was vigorously but ineffectually opposed by three Wigan defenders in the great winger's 40 yard solo dash for the line."

In the league, Hunslet visited Fartown on 8 October. Pat Devery dominated the game; he ran in four tries and kicked three goals in a 27–10 win. Lionel Cooper contributed the other two tries.

In the semi-final of the Yorkshire Cup, Huddersfield were drawn away to Dewsbury – Cooper scored a try in a 7–2 win – to set up a meeting with Bradford Northern in the final at Headingley on 29 October. It was a dour match and did not reach the heights of open rugby as expected; Huddersfield lost 11–4 to the cup holders.

Although the Fartowners had a fair share of possession from the scrum, Northern's forwards dominated the game, largely dictated the run of play and limited the amount of ball the classy Huddersfield backs had. Huddersfield were penalised at the first play-the-ball which enabled Bradford to get possession inside the Fartowners' half. Although Bradford won possession from the first two scrums, they made little headway against good Huddersfield tackling. Bradford created a scoring chance, but Walters made a mess of taking the pass before Ernest Ward was wide with a shot at goal after a play-the-ball offence by Huddersfield. Devery was also wide with a penalty kick 40 yards out. Davies regained some ground for Northern, and when Huddersfield were yet again penalised for a scrum infringement, Ernest Ward put Bradford ahead, only for Bawden to level the scores for a similar offence by Bradford.

A third goal came within the next minute, a poor pass by Daly gave Bradford the ball, Ernest Ward gathered it and dropped a goal from 30 yards out. The first glimpse of quality rugby came when Davies set his threequarters going, and opened out on the right to Batten who passed inside to Kitching only for him to spill the ball. So Northern went in at half-time 4–2 in front. Huddersfield had seen as much ball from the scrums as Bradford, but not until the closing stages of the half had they been able to show any sign of penetrating Bradford's defence. They made good ground early in the second half and when Donald Ward was penalised for feeding the scrum, Bawden levelled the scores.

Willie Davies began to come more and more into the picture and after Walters made a good break up the touchline, he took an inside pass and scored wide out. Ernest Ward failed with the conversion. Bradford began to pressurise Huddersfield and Ernest Ward put Bradford further ahead with another penalty. Huddersfield had a short spell on the attack, but Bradford were playing the better rugby and in reply to a Huddersfield drop-out Ernest Ward dropped a goal from a position 40 yards out to clinch the game for Bradford.

Huddersfield: E. Swallow, G. Wilson, J. Bawden, P.C. Devery, L.W. Cooper, G.R. Pepperell, W.M. Banks, J. Maiden, A.M. Meek, J.C. Daly, I.A. Owens, R. Nicholson, D.D. Valentine.
Scorer: Goals: Bawden 2.
Bradford Northern: W. Leake, E. Batten, E. Ward, J. Kitching, W. Walters, W.T.H. Davies, D. Ward, V.J. Darlison, R. Greaves, B. Tyler, T.J.F. Foster, K. Traill.
Scorers: Try: Davies. Goals: E. Ward 2. Drop-goals: E. Ward 2.
Referee: W. Hemmings (Halifax)
Attendance: 36,000 (£6,358)

At the beginning of December, A.N. Gaulton reviewed the Fartowners' season so far, and found they were "inconsistent". He continued: "Hunter still spends more time inside his opponents' '25' than any other full-back playing. This feature of his play causes great concern to the many purists in the Fartown crowd, but would it be wise to curb so ebullient a nature? The all-Australian left wing is still looked upon as the greatest danger-point by opponents...

"Devery has given us glimpses of the perfection of centre play, as witness that second-half against Hunslet at Fartown when he tore the Parksiders' defence to shreds. Similar exhibitions are all too rare."

The Fartowners were on the fringe of the top four places. Worryingly, there was a report that Hunter was going to return to Australia at the end of the season, although this turned out not to be correct and he signed a further contract to stay at Fartown. On 20 January 1950 *Rugby League Review* reported: "Balmain made a reasonable offer to Pat Devery to return home, but as with Easts and Hunter it appears they will have to manage without him. Easts had hopes of getting Johnny Hunter to stay in [Australia] when he returned from England, but news of his re-signing at Fartown has put an end to that."

Previewing the Challenge Cup matches, A.N. Gaulton said in *Rugby League Review*: "Devery and Cooper are, of course, known and respected wherever rugby league football is played. Each is a match-winner on his day and will not be given much latitude. Cooper will return all the keener after his few weeks' absence from the field of play and if the ball goes his way we shall see some thrills."

"Johnny Hunter will be at full-back. The Australian has turned the old term 'last line of defence' into 'last line of offence' and has shown us a new concept of full-back play. Some of his recent running up into the attack has been more judiciously tried than it was previously and the overlap has been more clear cut. There have been in the past, and there still are, great attacking full-backs in our game, but there's only one Johnny Hunter."

Huddersfield surprisingly went out early from the Challenge Cup, when they lost 13–8 on aggregate to Dewsbury in the first round. However, 11 games out of the next 13 were won. Cooper scored 13 tries in the last five of these to give him a season's total of 46. He was second in the national try-scorers list to Wigan's Brian Nordgren who had 57. Pat Devery managed 24 tries, and was joint 10th in the list.

Huddersfield finished second in the league, as well as winning the

Yorkshire League title for the 10th time since the competition started in 1907–08. Huddersfield's success in the Yorkshire League had been such that, allowing for the war periods when there was no championship, they had been either champions or runners-up every other year.

The Fartowners entertained Swinton in the semi-final play-off on 29 April 1950, and won 9–0 to progress to their second successive Championship Final, at Maine Road, Manchester, on 13 May 1950, this time against Wigan.

Wigan's 20–2 victory was one of the most sensational upsets ever seen in the domestic game. It was achieved without eight of their best players who were with Ernest Ward's Great Britain tour party in Australia.

Huddersfield had no players selected for the tour and had beaten a full Wigan side 27–8 a few weeks earlier on 4 March. The match had drawn a record attendance, 32,912, for a Huddersfield game at Fartown.

In the final, which drew a crowd of 65,065 despite Wigan's weakened state, Banks kicked off and, after only four minutes play, Wigan's captain, Ces Mountford, wrenched himself free from a tackle, cut through and passed to Silcock who went over in the corner. Silcock was playing on the wing; he was normally a second-row forward in the 'A' team. Ward added the goal with a fine kick. Wigan were dangerous again when Banks and Pepperell, trying the reverse pass, lost the ball. Wigan kicked on only for Cooper to collect the ball on his own line.

A penalty by Devery took Huddersfield upfield; however, the alert Nordgren intercepted a pass and raced 40 yards, outpacing Cracknell, to score after 15 minutes. Ward again landed the goal. Huddersfield began to assert themselves; Nicholson forced Wigan back 30 yards before passing to Cracknell who was held five yards from the corner flag.

A run by Pepperell gave Cooper a chance, but the winger was stopped inside the Wigan '25'. Huddersfield switched the attack to the right, but again Wigan's defence held firm. Great work by Hunter forced Wigan back again, but the Australian was unable to get his pass to Cracknell when the winger had a clear run through which left the score 10–0 to Wigan at the halfway stage.

After two minutes of the second half, Devery broke clear, kicked ahead and was obstructed. From the resultant penalty Bawden kicked a goal. Was it the start of a recovery from the Fartowners? Cooper regained possession and cut through the middle, but was well watched and the danger was nullified. For a while Wigan penned Huddersfield inside their own '25'; the Fartowners had plenty of ball, but could make no headway against tight Wigan marking; although relief came with a kick to touch.

Mountford made good ground for Wigan and Large took them to the Huddersfield line. A Fartown counterattack gave Cooper the chance to come infield and feed Hunter who was pushed into touch well inside Wigan's half. Penalties in favour of Huddersfield kept play on the Wigan line, Cracknell almost went over but on the intervention of the touch judge was called back and Wigan were given a penalty for obstruction.

Wigan went further ahead after Large had made an opening. Broome finished with a 40-yard run to go over for the try which Ward duly converted. In the final stages, Blan scored a late try for Wigan, and again Ward kicked the goal which finally shattered Huddersfield's hopes.

Huddersfield: J.C.H. Hunter, R. Cracknell, J. Bawden, P.C. Devery, L.W. Cooper, G.R. Pepperell, W.M. Banks, J.C. Daly, J. Mundy, A. Wilmot, K. Morrison, R. Nicholson, I.A. Owens.
Scorer: Goal: Bawden.
Wigan: E.H. Ward, N. Silcock, J. Broome, G. Roughley, B.C. Nordgren, C.R. Mountford, J. Alty, E. Slevin, H. McIntyre, F. Barton, W. Hudson, J. Large, W. Blan.
Scorers: Tries: Broome, Silcock, Nordgren, Blan. Goals: Ward 4.
Referee: Matt Coates (Pudsey)

The verdict on Huddersfield's 1949–50 season was given by "Autolycus" (Sidney H. Crowther) in the *Huddersfield Examiner:* "Huddersfield have to content themselves with being Yorkshire League Champions, runners-up in the Yorkshire Cup and runners-up in the League Championship.

The followers of many a club would think that a fine record, and will look to Fartown with a jealous eye, yet it might so easily have been better, the side having so much ability and played astonishing football, they really owed it to themselves to make the record better."

He went on: "Devery has given beautiful displays this season, showing himself to be possessed of every attribute of a class rugby player... he sees an opening a fraction of second sooner than anyone else."

Wakefield Trinity versus Huddersfield at Belle Vue on 29 March 1950. Lionel Cooper evades Wakefield defenders Froggatt and Fletcher to score.

Huddersfield 23 Leeds 15 at Fartown on 15 April 1950. In typical fashion, Cooper dives over to score his second try of the match.

Huddersfield 39 Bramley 5 at Fartown, first round Yorkshire Cup on 13 September 1950. Johnny Hunter breaks into the line to set up a passing movement. (Courtesy *Huddersfield Examiner*)

Huddersfield 16 Castleford 3, Yorkshire Cup Final at Headingley, 4 November 1950. Lionel Cooper, the Huddersfield captain, with the cup and Dick Cracknell and Russ Pepperell.

5. Yorkshire Cup winners

Inconsistency had been a feature of Huddersfield's play for the last couple of seasons; 1950–51 was again notable for the in-and-out form of the side. However, Huddersfield, under Cooper's captaincy, found a place on the honours list by winning the Yorkshire Cup.

Hunter had returned to Australia in the close season, and married Gwyn Vincent on 5 August at St Joseph's College in Sydney. He missed the first six games of the season.

Huddersfield did not retain the Yorkshire League title which had been theirs for the previous two seasons – 1950–51 was the first season since the war when they were not either champions or runners-up in the Yorkshire League – but the brilliant run in the forthcoming Yorkshire Cup competition was compensation for that. However, the team finished in a modest ninth position in the league table.

New Zealand rugby union threequarter Peter Henderson turned out to be another shrewd Fartown capture from overseas. He joined the club on 5 September 1950 – Huddersfield secured his signature in the face of strong opposition from St Helens, Leeds, Bradford Northern and Leigh – surprisingly, he had never seen a game of rugby league football.

He had made seven appearances for the All Blacks, and in the Empire Games held in Auckland in February 1950, represented his country in the 100-yard sprint and 110-yard sprint relay. In his first season he was a utility man, and filled the wing, centre and stand-off positions. He made 28 appearances and scored 14 tries. He added to the Fartowners' international make-up. On 13 October 1950 *Rugby League Review* reported that "Huddersfield can field a team with seven nationalities... but [also] had six players involved in the Cumberland versus Yorkshire [County Championship] match."

Early in the season Devery was in a great deal of discomfort due to a long-term groin injury, which gave him considerable pain during matches and immediately afterwards.

At one time he considered retiring – one medical report did not hold out more than a fifty–fifty chance of a cure. There was the possibility that an operation could leave a weakness. However, further specialist advice gave a more optimistic outlook.

Devery, who only the previous December had signed a new contract which would keep him at Fartown for the rest of his career, decided to have the operation. He was absent for two-thirds of the season and did not start playing again until 27 March 1951, and made only 17 appearances during the season.

The Yorkshire Cup run started with a first round aggregate score of 60–27 against Bramley. A 22–21 defeat at the Barley Mow, was followed by a 39–5 comprehensive win at Fartown. Cooper scored four tries.

In the second round, on 18 September, Huddersfield were drawn against Leeds at Headingley. A 29–2 win was far easier victory than anticipated. In the semi-final at Parkside on 6 October, Hunslet provided stronger opposition. They were overcome by a great display by Huddersfield – Hunter scored a try and Cooper got two in a 20–7 win.

Two days before, on Wednesday 4 October, a 1950 Australasian Tourist XIII played a Rest of the League XIII at Central Park, Wigan. The proceeds were donated to the late Lord Derby's Memorial Fund for the provision of playing fields on part of Lord Derby's estate at Knowsley. Cooper and Valentine were selected for the Rest, and Cooper scored a try in a 23–16 defeat.

On 4 November, Huddersfield appeared at Headingley as Yorkshire Cup finalists for the second year in succession. Castleford provided the opposition. A 16–3 win saw the Fartowners lift the cup for the 10th time since the competition started.

The game did not follow the pattern that was anticipated. Castleford no doubt intended to bottle up Cooper and his fellow winger Cracknell. They prevented either winger from scoring, so could claim that they succeeded in this. What happened, however, was that while the Castleford defence concentrated on blocking the way down the field via the touchlines, Huddersfield made inroads down the middle. Banks's lightning breaks down the centre caught out Castleford covering the wings, and had them on the wrong foot. Wagstaff had a good game for the Fartowners, but the whole pack played well in the loose as well as in the scrum; in the first half they won possession at a ratio of two to one.

After Huddersfield had kicked off, Castleford were penalised on the first play-the-ball and Bowden put the Fartowners ahead in the first minute. Castleford swept back with a cross-kick that found touch near the Huddersfield line. Huddersfield opened out play, but when Cracknell failed to hold a pass, the ball fell to Lloyd of Castleford who snapped it up to score. Langfield missed with the conversion.

Huddersfield kept up the attack with good forward play which was rewarded with a try from Pepperell who slipped through the Castleford defence on a thrilling 30-yard solo run to score between the posts. Bowden added the goal to make it 7–3 at the break.

The second half began with a Cooper break down the touchline, and when he was tackled Castleford were penalised for not retreating. Bowden increased the lead with the subsequent penalty. Banks, who was in devastating form, then cut through from his own '25' and fed Pepperell who outran the Castleford defence to score his second try. Bowden converted again.

A move involving Cooper and Owens swept down the field with some great interpassing, only for Castleford to be penalised again. Bowden landed his fifth goal, and now a Fartown victory was never in doubt.

Huddersfield: J.C.H. Hunter, R. Cracknell, J. Bowden, I.W. Clark, L.W. Cooper, G.R. Pepperell, W.M. Banks, F. Wagstaff, J. Mundy, A. Wilmot, R. Nicholson, I.A. Owens, D.D. Valentine.

Scorers: Tries: Pepperell 2. Goals: Bowden 5.

Castleford: R. Lewis , R.W. Lloyd, G. Broughton, P. Aldred, Brown, A. Fisher, G. Langfield, J. Anderson, J. Jones, J.L. Fleming, C. Howard, L. Haughey, F. Mugglestone.

Scorer: Try: Lloyd.

Referee: Ron Gelder (Wakefield)

Attendance: 28,610 (£5,148.)

Cooper enhanced his reputation by finishing the season with the second highest total of tries – 59 to Brian Bevan's 68. His total included scoring four tries in a match on five occasions. Hunter's unorthodox play earned him a total of 11 from the full-back position.

In December, *Rugby League Review* claimed that Bevan had been the first to 250 post-war tries and said that Cooper was the next highest on 195. However, their figures included matches that usually didn't count in the records, such as pre-season charity cup games. Cooper had scored the most in a match – eight against Yorkshire Amateurs in September 1948. Bevan had started playing for Warrington at the beginning of 1946–47, Cooper started six months later. A.N. Gaulton wrote that "Had there not been that time lag between the two, their try totals might well have been very similar."

In the Challenge Cup the Fartowners beat Whitehaven and Belle Vue Rangers before losing 2–0 to Wigan. Reviewing the club's campaign in *Rugby League Review*, A.N. Gaulton said: "Pat Devery was absent for two-thirds of the matches and was rarely the Devery of old upon his return... Considering the lengthy lean spell through which the team went, Cooper's total of 58 tries is a remarkable one... Cracknell, like Johnny Hunter, also had a troublesome time with injuries." [6]

---

[6] Cooper scored 59 tries overall in the season, 58 for Huddersfield, one for Other Nationalities.

The 1951–52 season was again notable for inconsistent form from the Huddersfield team. However, the Yorkshire League trophy came to Fartown and there was a place in the Championship play-offs. The side also scored more match points, 785, in the league than any other team.

Following a poor start in which both opening league games were lost, the team played erratically until the pack was strengthened by the signing of Ted Slevin and George Curran from Wigan, and Jack Brown from Salford. The team then found some consistent form, although there was an early exit from the Yorkshire Cup, going out in the second round 14–5 at Belle Vue to Wakefield Trinity.

Hunter's full-back play caught the eye, notably early in the season at Leigh on 22 August 1951, where he handed-off Trevor Allan in an amazing 75-yard run to score Huddersfield's only points in an 18–3 defeat.

Another typical Hunter try was at Hunslet on 29 September when an interception under his own posts produced a try from a length of the field run. Hunslet wingman Les Williams chased him, but could not catch him. Cooper scored a hat-trick of tries in the same game.

After Lionel Cooper had scored a hat-trick for Other Nationalities against France in a notoriously dirty game, he had another triumph for his club two weeks later. He scored 10 tries against Keighley at Fartown on 17 November. It was a record for the Huddersfield club, and beat fellow Australian Ray Markham's nine against Featherstone Rovers at Fartown on 21 September 1935. After the ninth try the announcer told the crowd that one more would be a club record, so there was great excitement when Cooper scored his tenth.

None of Cooper's 10 was the result of a walkover, at least seven of them were made after he had beaten three or more opponents; they were the reward for resolute running, promptitude and resource.

Banks had kicked off towards the pavilion end, and the game was only a minute old when Brereton was lectured and penalised for the way he had tried to stop Cooper. Huddersfield opened out and after two minutes of pressure on the Keighley line, Griffin fed Cooper who finished by scoring in the corner. Devery failed with the conversion.

An exchange of kicks between both full-backs ended when Dyson, who was standing in for Hunter, opened out play, but when Keighley were penalised a minute later – they were penalised three times in four scrums – Griffin increased the lead with a neat goal.

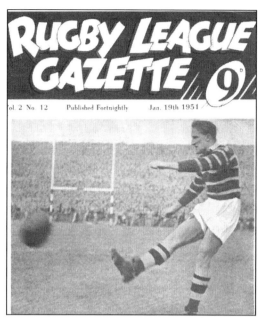

Pat Devery on the cover of *Rugby League Gazette*. The caption says: "Famous Huddersfield and Australian centre threequarter Pat Devery takes a shot at goal. This picture was taken last season. He has been unable to turn out this season due to his undergoing an operation from which he has not yet properly recovered. Every fan at Huddersfield and, indeed, every fan throughout the Rugby League, is hoping it will not be long before Pat is out again in the team. First class centres are too rare these days for the game to be deprived of the presence of such men."

Huddersfield 21 Whitehaven 9 at Fartown, Challenge Cup first round on 17 February 1951. Devery (No. 4) halts a Whitehaven attack, with Cooper, Daly and Hunter in support. Cooper scored four of Huddersfield's seven tries. (Courtesy *Huddersfield Examiner*)

A good run by Cracknell renewed the Huddersfield attack, and a burst by Cooper, who fell with three men on top of him, took Huddersfield to the Keighley line. Good work by Taylor and Redman drove Keighley well up the field, where the home side were penalised, de Lloyd was inches wide with his shot at goal. From then on it was all Huddersfield. Cooper lost the ball as he dodged through at the corner, but soon afterwards came inside from a scrum to go through under the posts. Incredibly Griffin failed with the conversion.

Another Huddersfield try came three minutes later. Cooper got the ball 35 yards from the line and beat three men to score in the corner. It was his third try in 25 minutes. Pepperell and Cracknell led the way back to the Keighley line; passes between Banks, Rylance and Devery ended when Pepperell scored the fourth try. Devery failed with the goalkick.

Again it was Cooper to the fore when Brown, who was making his Fartown debut, stole possession from a play-the-ball, and opened the way for the next score. The ball swung out to Banks and Rylance and then to Cooper, who finished the move by going over in the corner for his fourth try. Rylance tried his luck, but failed with the conversion.

The first half finished with the visitors attacking strongly near the Fartown line, but without success, so it was 17–0 at the interval. The five Huddersfield tries had been the result of fast and attractive play, with Cooper in devastating form, and as often as not more than a match for the opposition, but to their credit Keighley never gave up, although comprehensively outclassed.

In the second half, Huddersfield kept up the pressure on the Keighley line. Griffin made an opening for Cracknell to score wide out. Devery was not near enough with the conversion. It was one-way traffic. Cooper intercepted on the halfway line and went off on a run, although challenged by de Lloyd he pushed the full-back aside and scored in the corner. Devery missed the kick. Almost immediately, Rylance burst through the Keighley defence and passing by Banks, Pepperell and Devery ended with Cooper scoring his sixth try of the game. Griffin tried his luck again as goalkicker, but was no more fortunate than anyone else.

Keighley rallied when Mulhall tried hard to find a gap in the Fartown defence, but a 40-yard break by Cavanagh down the middle took play into the Keighley half, where Rylance intercepted and went through to score the ninth try. Cooper took the kick and added the two points.

Two minutes later Cooper scored his seventh try, but failed with the conversion. Brown made an opening for Cooper to finish with yet another try. This time he kicked the goal.

Huddersfield rugby league team 1951–52, winners of the Yorkshire League.
Back: Brian Heap, Dennis Cavanagh, Ike Owens, Bill Griffin, Jack Brown, Lionel
Cooper, George Curran, Ted Slevin, Peter Henderson; front: Dick Cracknell, Billy
Banks, Russ Pepperell (c), Frank Dyson, Ron Rylance, Pat Devery.

The next try scorer was Pepperell, after a move involving half the side.
Cooper failed with the kick. Keighley rallied and Britton scored a try, but
de Lloyd missed the kick.

Seven minutes from the end, Cooper equalled Markham's record,
bursting through on the open side of the scrum, and scored after a 45-
yard run to the line. Griffin failed with the kick. Three minutes before the
end, Cooper scored his 10th try and created a new record for the club.
Rylance this time failed with the goalkick. The match ended 48–3 – had
there been a more successful goalkicker on view the score would have
been much wider.

Cooper's match tally of 34 points fell short of a club record – Major
Holland kicked 18 goals and scored a try against Swinton Park in a
Challenge Cup match at Fartown in 1914 for a total of 39, while Jeff
Bawden scored five tries and kicked 10 goals for 35 points against
Swinton at Fartown on 13 April 1946.

Huddersfield: F. Dyson, R. Cracknell, G.R. Pepperell, P.C. Devery, L.W. Cooper,
R. Rylance, W.M. Banks, W.D. Cavanagh, J. Mundy, W.A. Griffin, J. Brown,
E. Slevin, D.D. Valentine.

Keighley: De Lloyd, Buckley, Taylor, Prescott, Ivill, Redman, Barrett, Brereton,
Britton, J.V. Smith, Mulhall, Bedford, Kelly.

Referee: T Watkinson (Manchester)

Attendance: 9,496

The Challenge Cup again was a disappointment for the Fartowners,
who were knocked out by Halifax in the first round. At the beginning of

February Huddersfield beat Castleford 24–7. *Rugby League Review* commented that "Having four or five men detailed to watch Cooper is all very well, but it leaves a gap or two elsewhere." Despite this, Cooper still scored a hat-trick of tries.

On Saturday 8 March 1952, Doncaster paid their first ever visit to Fartown. The new club had a remarkable first season and eventually finished11th in the final table. Earlier in the season at Doncaster on 13 October 1951, Huddersfield had been lost 18–10. On this occasion, however, the Fartowners outclassed their opponents 34–10 before a crowd of 10,145.The match was significant because Pat Devery landed eight goals and Lionel Cooper scored his 60th try of the season. The liveliness of Banks, playing at stand-off, Devery's fine goalkicking and good backing up by the Huddersfield forwards were also features of the game. St Helens provided strong opposition at Fartown on Easter Monday and seldom looked as inferior as the 34–15 score suggested. In midfield their forwards, among whom Prescott was outstanding, were always a handful. What they lacked, however, was fitness and pace to contend with the Fartown pack where Valentine and Griffin were in great form, backed by Slevin and Curran.

Saints' left flank was the more dangerous, but found difficulty matching Henderson's speed. On the other wing, Huddersfield had a big advantage in Cooper, who was in devastating form. The Australian scored five tries, in one of which he beat four successive attempts at a tackle. These tries by Cooper brought his total for the season to 69, two better than Brian Bevan's post-war record of 67.

There was a fine finish to the season in which 11 of the last 12 league games were won to ensure Huddersfield fourth place in the table and a semi-final play-off at Odsal against Bradford Northern on 3 May 1952.

Despite a gallant closing rally, Huddersfield failed by the narrow margin of 18–15 to reach the Championship Final. In front of a crowd of 56,400, Bradford's powerful pack was the deciding factor. They harassed Huddersfield into too many bad passes and the Fartowners dropped the ball too often when under pressure.

Despite this, Huddersfield deserved credit for their determined second half rally in which Henderson played a great part. With Northern 10–4 to the good at half-time, he scored twice and neither was an easy try. However, in between his tries McClean and Mageen raced in for tries to keep Bradford comfortably in control, although after Valentine dived over for a third Huddersfield try and Cavanagh kicked the goal, the Fartowners were three points behind in a game which could have gone either way.

Throughout the season, Frank Dyson proved a very capable deputy to Hunter, while there was a surplus of riches for the wing positions with Cooper, Cracknell and Henderson vying for the two places, each was a match-winner in his own right. Injuries had handicapped Devery and Pepperell – Rylance had been signed as a stand-off, but with Devery out of action he proved to be a valuable centre, and played many of his games there. Late in the season, Billy Banks moved to stand-off with Peter Bates as his partner, which proved to be a lively combination.

The forwards got stronger as the season progressed. Valentine was, as ever, at the forefront of everything, while the three Lancastrians, Slevin, Brown and Curran gave the pack some consistency.

Individually, pride of place went to Lionel Cooper who scored more tries in a season than ever before and topped the national try-scoring charts with 71. He was eight in front of his nearest rival, Bradford Northern's New Zealander Jack McClean. Cracknell, with 47 tries, and Henderson, with 31, were also high up in the list.

As well as Cooper's five tries against St Helens on Easter Monday, he scored four tries in a match twice and ran in hat-tricks of tries six times. In April he had passed 300 tries, and seemed to have a chance of breaking Rosenfeld's record of 80 tries in a season. He finished on 71, although he was usually heavily marked in matches. A.N. Gaulton pointed out that he "never looked or called for 'spoon fed' tries." He also said that had Pat Devery been fit throughout the season, and been Cooper's regular partner at centre, Cooper almost certainly would have passed Rosenfeld's record.

Gaulton felt that the season had mixed "brilliance and mediocrity" for Huddersfield's supporters, but was optimistic for the future, and felt that Jack Large was an important signing to strengthen the pack.

Pat Devery kicks for goal.

6. A Wembley triumph

The year 1953 saw Princess Elizabeth crowned Queen, Mount Everest conquered, Stanley Matthews win his first FA Cup winners medal at the age of 38 and, after 28 attempts Sir Gordon Richards won the Derby on Pinza.

Rugby league also enjoyed a golden spell – none more so than at Huddersfield who had slowly, but surely, produced another great team which started to pay dividends.

A pre-season message from Wilf Stoker, the chairman of the club's Football Committee, in the *Huddersfield Examiner* of Saturday 16 August 1952 outlined: "Huddersfield's work in post-war Rugby League football is such that the majority of League clubs would be very pleased and proud to have done equally as well.

During this period they have enhanced the club's traditional reputation for high class and often brilliant displays, despite occasional disappointments and failures in certain matches...Supporters of Fartown, however, demand almost as their birthright the provision for this type of football, and at the dawn of a new season, future prospects are of more interest than past glories. Questions such as 'Is this to be our year?' 'Are we for Wembley?' 'Can we win all four?' are frequently heard."

The questions and optimism expressed wasn't too far off the mark at the end of an eventful 1952–53 season. Other than the close season signing of Jack Large, a second-rower from Wigan, the team sheet read pretty much as it did the previous April and March.

After the first couple of league games, Huddersfield were on the Yorkshire Cup trail. In the first round, first leg at Fartown, Huddersfield took on Hunslet, who had finished ninth in the league the previous season. Devery kicked five goals in a close-fought 19–14 win: a narrow lead to take to Parkside. The second leg saw Huddersfield at their best. Cooper scored two tries in an 18–2 victory.

On 20 September 1952, Huddersfield travelled to Craven Park and trounced struggling Hull KR 44–10. The Fartowners were never extended in their task of compiling 44 points, although in the second half Hull KR did briefly interrupt Huddersfield's rate of scoring.

"Autolycus" in the *Huddersfield Examiner* wrote: "Most of the scoring was done by Cooper, he had seven tries in all, some of them finished at a gentle trot and some accomplished by the summary dismissal of consecutive or concerted tackles.

63

At first the home crowd groaned at the spectacle of what they called weak tackling, and then, before the end, were clamouring for the repetition of the spectacle of Cooper going all out for the line...they barracked Devery for taking a kick at goal 40 yards out because they wanted 'football'." Griffin, Rylance and Henderson were the other try-scorers, and Devery kicked seven goals.

The second round of the Yorkshire Cup saw Huddersfield drawn away to Hull. Hull had finished third the previous season, with one more point than the Fartown side.

Huddersfield's forwards harassed the opposition to the extent that Hull could not get into their stride, and the home defence was unable to cope when the Fartown backs opened out at pace with swift, accurate passing. Once again Huddersfield pulled out their best on away territory to win 29–7.Most of the try scoring was done by Cooper, with four, to go with those of Large, Devery and Henderson. Devery added four goals.

Gales and rain dominated Huddersfield's Yorkshire Cup semi-final against Halifax at Fartown on 13 October. Halifax had finished 21st in the table in 1951–52, but improved dramatically this season to eventually take second place in the table.

Halifax had the wind behind them in the first half and did virtually all the attacking. Loose-forward Clarkson kicked three goals, and Hopkins got a foot to the ball and followed it over the line for a try.

A beautiful cut-through by Large promised well in the first half, but he held on too long with men well placed on his shoulder waiting for the offload. Another run by Banks augured well, but his long pass to Cooper missed its mark. These two efforts were Huddersfield's only attacks, other than that the first half was all Halifax.

There were two differences between the first half and the second. Halifax were without Clarkson for the first 20 minutes of the second half after he collided with Valentine at the kick-off. He was carried off unconscious and did not return until the later stages.

The other difference was Halifax, against the strong wind, had more of the ball and controlled it better. When Huddersfield did get the ball they dropped passes too often. With the support of the wind, Huddersfield improved, but their attempts to open out passing were defeated either by the close Halifax covering or their poor handling.

They did, however, manage to find a way through Halifax's defence. Their try was similar to the one Halifax scored. Devery followed a kick through over the line to score. Devery's three goals – the final one a last-minute equaliser – tied the score at 9–9, with a replay necessary at Thrum Hall three days later.

Huddersfield had to call up five reserves, but they rose to the occasion in grand style as they beat Halifax 15–5 in the replay. The game was only three minutes old when Bawden opened the scoring for Huddersfield with a penalty, but two minutes later Halifax were on the Fartown line where Rylance lost the ball only for Kielty to snap it up and dive over.

Sullivan, on the left wing in place of Cooper, had a couple of good runs then Brown was pulled down just short of the line after taking a cross-kick by Pepperell. Rylance had two shots at goal from penalties. The second one was successful after 28 minutes, which gave Huddersfield a lead they never lost. Shortly after that, Banks sent Sullivan in for a try to make the half-time score 7–3 to the Fartowners. After five minutes of the second half a goal by Clarkson narrowed the gap to two points before Dyson, who was standing in for Hunter, scored a try following good work by Banks who cut through on the blind side. Dyson finished the move in the corner. However, Rylance missed the kick. Clarkson missed penalty then, with eight minutes left, Rylance kicked a fine goal to clinch Huddersfield's place in the final.

Australia were the visitors to Fartown on Saturday 1 November as part of their 1952–53 tour. Many pundits thought that Huddersfield, who had won 13 out of their 16 league and Yorkshire Cup matches so far, would inflict a second defeat in a club game on the tourists. This was not to be and the Australians won 27–9.

The first half was one of fast and furious rugby, with both teams evenly matched in speed and handling ability. The tourists went in at half-time with a 12–5 lead. Huddersfield started the second half in a determined mood and it seemed that the strong pressure they applied on the Australian defence would eventually bring them the points to at least level the scores. However, it was the opportunism and backing up which featured so largely in Australia's play that turned the tables on the Fartowners.

First, Hazzard raced away to score after picking up a pass dropped by Rylance, then Collinson and Flannery profited from Huddersfield handling errors. Churchill kicked six goals, with the other Australian tries scored by Carlson and Davies. However, Huddersfield could have had three more tries as well as the one scored by Rylance and improved by Devery – who kicked three goals in all – had Pepperell,

Devery and Large chosen to pass to unmarked colleagues in attacking movements. A.N. Gaulton commented in *Rugby League Review* that "Three of the Australian tries were gifts". The Australians never let up in the robustness of their play, but were met by some resolute tackling, in particular by Henderson and Hunter.

Huddersfield: J.C.H. Hunter, P. Henderson, R. Rylance, P.C. Devery, L.W. Cooper, G.R. Pepperell (c), W.M. Banks, E. Slevin, G. Curran, W. Griffin, J. Brown, J. Large, D.D. Valentine.

Australia: C. Churchill(c), D. Flannery, N. Hazzard, C. Geelan, B. Carlson, F. Stanmore, C. Donohoe, D. Hall, K. Schubert, C. Gill, B. Davies, T. Tyrrell, A. Collinson.

Referee: Stan. Adams (Hull)

Attendance: 25,490 (£3,450)

Huddersfield appeared in their 18th Yorkshire Cup Final at Headingley on Saturday 16 November when their opponents were Batley, who had last won the cup in 1912. Batley were traditionally not one of Yorkshire's strongest sides, but had finished the previous season in 17th place in the league, and had beaten Dewsbury, Keighley and Featherstone Rovers to reach the final.

The attendance of 15,500 was undoubtedly affected by fog, although the referee, C.F. Appleton of Warrington, was never in a position to have to call the game off. The murky sky and visibility were just about good enough to play. However, *Rugby League Review*, which was often critical of the RFL, said that the game had kicked off at 3pm, and that it had been very dark for much of the second half.

Batley kicked off and a return kick to touch by Pepperell put the Fartowners well inside the Batley half. When Huddersfield were penalised Walshaw was wide with a shot at goal, but a further penalty against Huddersfield helped Batley keep up the pressure on the Fartown line. A run by Cooper took play back to the middle, then a burst by Pepperell found a hole in the Batley defence – Pepperell kicked through but was obstructed; Devery opening the scoring with a fine goal after nearly 10 minutes play.

Batley responded with a move from the scrum to Etty's wing, then lost possession when Huddersfield got to the ball first, Henderson taking the Fartowners into the Batley 25 yard line area.

Huddersfield opened out towards Cooper who was stopped a yard short of the line; Cooper however, played the ball forward, and got the touch for a try before the defence could do anything to stop him. Devery missed with the conversion.

Batley were strong opponents. They had as much of the play as Huddersfield and their close marking broke up promising Fartown attacks. Batley changed their direction of attack and when Banks was penalised a scrum offence, Walshaw missed a fairly easy shot at goal.

Huddersfield went further ahead with another Cooper try; the opening was made by Ramsden who sent out a wide pass for Cooper to score. Devery missed the conversion. A minute later Devery kicked a penalty, but Batley replied with a try from Etty. Walshaw missed the goal kick, so Huddersfield had a 10–3 half-time lead.

Almost immediately on the resumption, Devery failed with a long-range shot at goal. Batley gained some ground with an interception and worked their way up field; Etty had a couple of good runs, but was not allowed to go far. A kick and follow-up took Batley to the Fartowners' line, before Large broke away, but a promising move was halted because of a forward pass. Visibility was deteriorating rapidly, but in the gloom Cooper scored his third try, again Devery missed with the conversion. The conditions were grim for the spectators, but not for Batley as Kenny went in for a try goaled by Laycock to bring them within five points of Huddersfield. However, soon Valentine scored a try following a Henderson run and Devery kicked the goal to make it 18–8 to make the game safe for Huddersfield.

The *Yorkshire Post* commented: "Because of their speed, Huddersfield pulled out passing moves which Batley could not match...no-one but Cooper could have scored three of their tries, particularly the second when he had Harrison, Walshaw and Laycock all trying to claw him down over the last eight yards to the line."

Vincent Firth in *Rugby League Review* commented: "...Notwithstanding all their gameness, their dash and their perseverance, Batley never looked like lifting the trophy. The reason for their defeat is not far to seek and can be summed up in one word – class."

Huddersfield: J.C.H. Hunter, P. Henderson, P. Ramsden, P.C. Devery, L.W. Cooper, G.R. Pepperell (c), W.M. Banks, E. Slevin, G. Curran, W. Griffin, J. Brown, J. Large, D.D. Valentine.
Scorers: Tries: Cooper 3, Valentine. Goals: Devery 3.
Batley: P. Walshaw, G. Harrison, G. Kenny, W. Riches, J. Etty, W. Riley, R.C. Laycock (c), H. Wagstaff, H. McIntyre, T. Jones, G. Palmer, C. Briggs, J. Westbury.
Scorers: Tries: Kenny, Etty. Goal: Laycock.
Referee: C.F. Appleton (Warrington)
Attendance: 15,000 (£2,448)

Huddersfield, who had the Yorkshire Cup in their trophy cabinet, turned their attention towards the Challenge Cup, and in the First Round were drawn against Castleford.

With first-leg ground advantage at Fartown on Saturday 7 February 1953, Huddersfield built up a 22 point lead, winning 36–14. Castleford played with plenty of life, but the Fartowners held out at the most critical stages, and basically were most effective when pressed in their own '25'. At least four of Huddersfield's eight tries were scored from movements that started not far from their own line.

The running of Henderson, who had three tries, and Cooper who had four, played a considerable part in the victory, but the influence of the centres Devery and Pepperell was also important. They did valuable work, particularly in the second half. In addition to scoring a try, Devery kicked six goals.

The game was significant for the fact that Cooper scored his 1,000th point for the Claret and Gold and in doing so became the fifth Fartowner to reach such a total. His predecessors were Ben Gronow, Albert Rosenfeld, Alex Fiddes and Jeff Bawden.

The end of a hard-fought second leg at Wheldon Road left Huddersfield easily the aggregate victors on 14 February. A 6–2 win gave an overall score of 42–16. The heavy ground narrowed the difference between the two sides. With a lot of possession, Castleford were able to give Huddersfield something of a gruelling time, their forwards in particular were good at slipping the ball out when tackled.

The Huddersfield half-backs, Ramsden and Banks, had the edge over their counterparts Batten and Pye and this had a great deal to do with Huddersfield's 6–2 win. Cooper scored the Fartowners' two tries; Devery, however, found the heavy ball too great a handicap to add any points from kicks.

A 21–7 home win over Barrow in the second round at Fartown on 28 February brought young stand-off Peter Ramsden into the spotlight. The *Sunday Graphic* wrote: "Six tries, everyone a gem. Victory went to the better side, yet few will disagree that up to the interval Barrow were definitely on top. The man, or should I say boy who put them on the road to victory was 18-year-old out-half Peter Ramsden. Fastening on to a Banks pass he brushed maestro Willie Horne to one side, streaked through the gap, doubled inside the full-back and dived over with Castle making a desperate attempt to stop him. That burst was a memory-kindler of Vic Hey over the same distance and it was the tonic the Fartowners needed."

Huddersfield's other try scorers in front of a crowd of 25,608 were Cooper, who got two, Pepperell and Devery. Devery added three goals. Barrow's points were from a Castle try with two goals by Horne.

Huddersfield's forwards were in great form in the third round tie against Bradford Northern at Odsal on 14 March. A packed crowd of 69,198 saw Slevin and Valentine play a key role for the Fartowners in a 17–7 win which put them into the semi-final.

They had untiring support from Curran who lead the pack well, plus a non-stop performance from Bowden in the front-row. Huddersfield were desperate to lay the Bradford bogey, because Northern often had the upper hand over the Fartowners. The home side showed they meant business early on when McLean scored a try – the only time it could be said that Bradford had anything like ascendancy in the match. However, the game still looked to be in Northern's favour as Huddersfield reached half-time a point down at 5–4.

Huddersfield came more into their own after the interval and following a period of play on the Bradford line, Banks found a gap to score a try. The Fartown supporters' worries were eased when Cracknell went in for another try, then a Banks drop-goal and a further try from Cracknell rubbed salt into Bradford's wounds.

Devery landed three goals and covered well in open play, while Pepperell's guile at centre often confused the Bradford defence. Hunter took the ball well at full-back, but the strength and quality of the Huddersfield pack in front of him won the day for the Fartowners.

There was now the possibility of Huddersfield becoming the first post-war team to win 'All four Cups', the Challenge Cup, Championship, Yorkshire Cup and Yorkshire League.

Huddersfield returned to Odsal for the semi-final. A heavy ground, slippery ball and a high wind were the factors both Huddersfield and Wigan had to contend with on Saturday 28 March. Forty minutes before the start there was a fresh downpour of rain which left standing pools of water on the pitch. However, the weather did not deter the fans with a turnout of 58,772.

The first half produced an end-to-end struggle, although each side found the ball difficult to handle. Huddersfield were at a disadvantage 20 minutes after the start when Pepperell had to leave the field with blood streaming down his face. He had two stitches inserted in a head wound before returning to the play a minute before half-time with his head bandaged under a scrum cap.

There was not much to choose between the sides as they went in

0–0 at the interval. Wigan were first on the attack after the break, and were inside the Huddersfield half, with the issue fought out by the two sets of forwards.

As in the third round, it was the Fartown pack that began to gain advantage. The opening score came out of the blue after nine minutes of play in the second half when Henderson reached half-way and cross-kicked. Pepperell just failed to get to the bounce and Wigan full-back Cunliffe let the ball run over the line. Valentine touched down for a try under the posts; Devery converted.

Both sets of forwards soon resumed their private duel, with Slevin, Large, Curran and Valentine outstanding for Huddersfield. After a run and cross-kick by Brian Nordgren raised Wigan's hopes, Slevin and Valentine worked their way back into the Wigan '25'. Here, five minutes from the end, Devery increased Huddersfield's lead with a penalty after Wigan had strayed offside to make the final score 7–0.

Vincent Firth concluded: "Huddersfield have been Cup favourites since the first round and in this game they played like favourites just as they did against Bradford Northern. Wigan offered powerful opposition but they were simply no match for the Fartowners, whose team-blend was truly great."

Huddersfield made their third appearance at Wembley and their seventh in a Challenge Cup Final when they met St Helens on Saturday 25 April 1953. It was Huddersfield's first visit to Wembley since 1933.

April was certainly a busy month for the 'claret and gold' for they completed nine fixtures in that period and no one complained. The week prior to the final not one player was rested, and the team which was to turn out at Wembley beat Wigan at Fartown 17–10.

Wembley was new ground for the majority of players on both sides, particularly for those who had come to Huddersfield from Australia and New Zealand. Nearly all the players in the Huddersfield team had gained international, test match or county honours, but only Slevin and Curran had played before in a Wembley final and that was with Wigan.

The three Australians were still key players in a Huddersfield side full of quality players. *Rugby League Review's* match preview said that Johnny Hunter was "still a great attraction wherever Huddersfield play. He may be a little slower than he was a year or two ago, and perhaps his natural enthusiasm is now tempered with a little more discretion than of old – but there's still only one Johnny Hunter. A wonderful catcher of a ball at any angle and a 'safe as houses' tackler."

Pat Devery was described as the 'marksman' of the side and "At his best, Devery is one of the cleverest centres in the game today – graceful in movement, elusive in running and quick to spot the half-opening. His effectiveness does not end there either, for he is also strong on defence and rarely misses his man in the tackle."

Lionel Cooper was said to be "the hero of nearly all the small boys in Huddersfield – and many of the adults as well. Continues to score try after try despite the close marking of innumerable opponents. His strength and determination count for a great deal, but that he uses his physical powers fairly is shown by his great popularity with spectators on many grounds outside Fartown."

Saints were favourites to win the Cup having finished top of the league table. It had been a great season for them. They had gone through the season without defeat away from home.

The RFL banned television coverage of the final, fearing that it would hit the attendance, but did allow match commentary on the Home Service of BBC Radio. However, this did not deter both sets of fans from Lancashire and Yorkshire contributing to a crowd of 89,588 at Wembley.

The Final, however, was controversial. The Lancastrians had clearly decided on a physical approach towards Huddersfield's attacking play, the majority of the large crowd was so incensed that they consistently booed the Saints side. However, in a game which contained some excellent rugby, along with a considerable amount of rough play, Saints met their match. Vincent Firth said that "I have never seen any Northern League club engage in a more provocative game than the St Helens team did against Huddersfield". He also said that St Helens were booed at the end of the game.

The first points went on the board after 29 minutes when Ramsden took a pass from Slevin, ignored a two-man overlap and broke a tackle by Prescott to go on his own and scramble over the line near enough for Devery to convert. Saints claimed that Ramsden had grounded the ball short, but referee Phillips, of Widnes, awarded the try.

When it appeared that the Fartowners would go in at the break 5–0 ahead, Langfield kicked a penalty goal and from the restart a length-of-the-field move involved three Saints players before wingman Steve Llewellyn raced down the touchline and rounded Hunter to score an unconverted try. So the teams went in level at 5–5.

Huddersfield applied the early pressure in the second half. Cooper, Henderson and Ramsden went close, but for all their endeavours they failed to crack the Saints defence.

It was against the run of play when Saints scored and took the lead in the 59th minute. Llewellyn and Greenall broke from half-way and put Langfield in near the posts. Although the conversion was not difficult, Langfield failed to add the extra points and Saints' lead was just three points at 8–5.Hunter was then carried off after being tackled off the ball by Llewellyn. A leg injury forced Devery onto the wing for most of the second half. However, this failed to deter the Fartowners who were causing the Saints defence problems with strong attacks.

A scrum was won near the Saints' posts and from the heel Banks shot over to level the scores. Cooper landed the conversion to restore Huddersfield's lead. In the 72nd minute Langfield manoeuvred into position to drop a goal for St Helens and it was 10–10. To the delight of the crowd Hunter returned and four minutes later in the 76th minute Bowden and Valentine cut through downfield and interpassed until Ramsden, in support, took a great pass from Bowden to romp over for the winning try.

Cooper converted and in the last minute went in under the posts only to be brought back for a forward pass before referee George Phillips blew the final whistle to make it 15–10 and start the celebrations for Fartown.

The Fartowners were a wounded, but elated, bunch of players after 80 minutes, even more so when Peter Ramsden on his 19th birthday received the Lance Todd Trophy as man-of-the-match.

Huddersfield: J.C.H. Hunter, P. Henderson, G.R. Pepperell (c), P.C. Devery, L.W. Cooper, P. Ramsden, W.M. Banks, E. Slevin, G. Curran, J. Bowden, J. Brown, J. Large, D.D. Valentine.
Scorers: Tries: Ramsden 2, Banks. Goals: Cooper 2, Devery.
St Helens: A.G. Moses, S.M. Llewellyn, D. Greenall (c), D. Gullick, S. McCormick, J. Honey, G. Langfield, A.G. Prescott, R.E. Blakemore, G. Parr, G. Parsons, W. Bretherton, W.R. Cale.
Referee: G.S. Phillips (Widnes)
Attendance: 89,588 (£30,865)

Pat Devery was a teacher at Oakes Elementary School in Huddersfield. Asked in 2009 about Huddersfield's appearance in the Challenge Cup Final that year, he recalled: "Some of the lads stayed in London after the 1953 Final, but I had to get back to Huddersfield, the people at Oakes School would not let me have any time off."

Having just missed out on the Yorkshire League title by one point to Halifax, it was an exhausted Huddersfield playing squad which finished the 1952–53 season. They had to play their final 13 games in 36 days of which they won nine, lost three and drew one. They finished fourth in the league table, which meant a trip to St Helens in the play-off semi-final. Saints took revenge for their Wembley defeat, walloped Huddersfield 46–0, and went on to beat Halifax 24–4 in the final at Maine Road.

The St Helens crowd took great pleasure at their side's victory at the expense of Huddersfield at Knowsley Road on 2 May – the crowd had, of course, every right to feel delighted. Not only was the result some consolation for the Cup Final defeat, but Saints' play, over the past season, had seldom looked as good as it did against Huddersfield.

The *Huddersfield Examiner* commented: "Only against such sides as Liverpool or Bramley can the Saints have had so easy a passage, and being fully alert, completely fit and full of enthusiasm they were able to play fast, open football of an exhilarating character.

Huddersfield were lifeless, there were times when it seemed that as much they could do was to drag one leg after another. Ramsden who, after all, has had a week's rest, sometimes livened up the attack. Banks whipped himself up to one fine effort, but no-one was at hand to help. Hunter also showed occasional flashes, Cooper came very near to a score, but he also lacked support, and Henderson was plainly trying, but too well watched by a fresher opponent.

It seemed symbolical of Huddersfield's general state when Valentine once got the ball and then gave every sign of wondering whatever to do with it. That was Huddersfield's trouble – there was no freshness in them, they played as a side who were suffering from brain fag and from being leg weary, and the former counted as much as the latter, for they were slow in thinking as well as slow in moving."

Even so, it had been a wonderful season for Huddersfield securing both the Yorkshire and Rugby League Challenge Cups, individually Cooper, with 50 tries, and Henderson, with 46, finished well up in the national leading try scorers table. Devery kicked 145 goals in all games, which was only beaten by Harry Bath and George Langfield. More significantly for the Fartowners, he amassed 332 points from 16 tries and 142 goals – to this day a Huddersfield club record for points in a season. Only Harry Bath, who amassed 379, beat him.

Wembley 1953

At the railway station before going to Wembley. From left: Billy Banks, Peter Ramsden, Johnny Hunter, Russ Pepperell, Jack Large, George Curran, Ron Rylance, Jim Cooper, Dick Cracknell, Jack Brown, Ted Slevin, Dave Valentine, Wilf Stoker (Football Committee Chairman). (Courtesy Michael O'Hare)

Huddersfield players at Wembley 1953: Pat Devery, Johnny Hunter, Russ Pepperell, Dick Cracknell, Lionel Cooper, Peter Ramsden, Peter Henderson, Ron Rylance.

74

Captains Russ Pepperell (Huddersfield) and Duggie Greenall (St Helens) lead the teams out onto the field. Huddersfield players (left to right): Johnny Hunter, Peter Henderson, Pat Devery, Lionel Cooper, Peter Ramsden, Billy Banks, Ted Slevin. (Courtesy *Huddersfield Examiner*)

Huddersfield 15 St Helens 10, Challenge Cup Final at Wembley on 25 April 1953. Huddersfield captain, Russ Pepperell, introduces Pat Devery to the Duke of Norfolk prior to the game. Other Fartowners are Peter Ramsden, Lionel Cooper and Peter Henderson. (Courtesy *Huddersfield Examiner*)

Pat Devery brings down Saints winger Llewellyn assisted by Jack Large (left) and Lionel Cooper (right). George Curran looks on.

Huddersfield scrum-half Billy Banks about to take the ball out of the scrum as referee George Phillips (Widnes) blows up for an infringement.
(Courtesy Michael O'Hare)

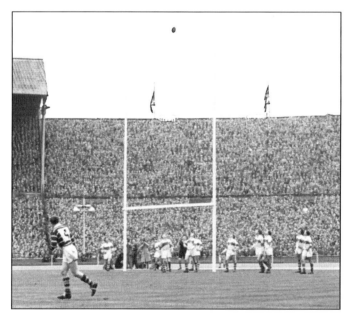
Pat Devery converts Peter Ramsden's second try at Wembley.

Huddersfield captain, Russ Pepperell, receives the Challenge Cup from
His Grace the Duke of Norfolk.

Amid scenes of jubilant Fartown supporters, Huddersfield captain Russ
Pepperell makes his way back down onto the pitch with the cup, followed by
Jack Brown. (Courtesy *Huddersfield Examiner*)

Bringing the Cup home.
(Courtesy Michael O'Hare)

Huddersfield rugby league team 1952–53. Winners of the Challenge Cup and Yorkshire Cup. Back: Committee: J.T. Withers, W. Cunningham, H. Lockwood, J. Wood-Beever, H.V. Wood (president), W. Stoker, B. Gronow, T. Matthewman, Arthur Archbell (secretary); middle: H. Tiffany (assistant trainer), J. Brown, W. Griffin, J. Bowden, J. Large, J. Cooper, E. Slevin, D.D. Valentine, J. Waring (masseur), W. Smith (trainer); seated: R. Cracknell, P. Henderson, J. Hunter, R. Pepperell (c), L. Cooper, P. Devery, R. Rylance; front: W. Banks, P. Ramsden; inset: G. Curran.

7. Pat Devery retires

What of Huddersfield in 1953–54? The forwards had given many striking performances in the previous season, with one of the best front-row formations they had found for years. With Bowden, Curran, Slevin, Brown, Griffin and Valentine still available, along with the acquisition of Charlie Armitt from Swinton, the pack still looked formidable.

Russ Pepperell was reappointed as player-coach in July 1953, but a big shock was a letter of resignation from Lionel Cooper. Changes are inevitable, but it seemed strange that at the age of 30 so resolute a player, still in full training, should have been thinking of retiring. The threat did not seem serious enough for him not to start the season. Huddersfield won three out of the first four league games with Cooper in the side, and he played on for another two seasons, thoughts of retirement forgotten. Business commitments may have been behind his thoughts of retiring.

Two of Yorkshire's formidable cup-fighting sides, Huddersfield and Wakefield Trinity, met at Fartown on 5 September for the 15th time in Yorkshire Cup matches. The Fartowners were determined to level the number of successes by each side. Of the previous 14 games Huddersfield had won six, Wakefield seven, with one draw. In fact since the end of the war, Wakefield and Huddersfield had monopolised the competition with the exception of the 1948 and 1949 successes by Bradford Northern. In all, Huddersfield had won the cup 11 times to Wakefield's five.

Huddersfield were defending the trophy, and it was the Fartowners who took a big lead into the second leg. Devery kicked 10 goals in a 47–9 win. Huddersfield's workmanlike display was at times interspersed with magnificent passing and running. Wakefield were renowned for having the heaviest pack in rugby league, but the game showed that weight is not necessarily the only attribute of a good pack of forwards.

Weight itself will not force an opening through a strong defence such as Huddersfield's, and it was no match for some determined running by Valentine, clever positioning by Armitt and all-round solid work by the remaining forwards who in the end completely subdued the Trinity pack.

The forwards had paved the way for the Fartowners' backs to produce quick bouts of passing and powerful running that had Wakefield's defence on the wrong foot on numerous occasions. It has to be said that Wakefield were badly affected by injuries – Huddersfield too had their misfortunes in this respect – and it hardly seemed a wise move to put Mortimer at full-back when Luckman, who had been concussed in a collision with Valentine, went onto the wing, because he was clearly the main attacking force in the visiting backs. The move to full-back restricted his chances.

Banks caused big problems for the Trinity defence, and Devery and Henderson often made light of the attempts to stop them. The home backs ran in the tries – Henderson got a hat-trick, Rylance scored twice and Bowden, Banks, Cooper and Armitt all scored as well for Huddersfield. Boocker, Luckman and Froggett replied for Wakefield.

In the second leg at Belle Vue on 9 September, the Fartowners did not have it their own way and lost 20–7. Pepperell scored a try along with two goals from Devery. However, an aggregate score of 54–29 took them safely through to the second round.

David Rose, a Scottish rugby union international, had signed from Jedforest RFC on 29 August 1953.Scottish borders rugby union had been a good recruitment area for the Fartown club and he made his first appearance in a claret and gold jersey in place of Pepperell at Fartown on 19 September against Hull KR.

It was another high scoring game, with Cooper and Devery to the fore in a 47–8 win. Rovers were not as poor as the scoreline suggested. They were first to score through wingman Knapp and for 15 minutes kept Huddersfield subdued, but they lacked the forwards who could stay the pace. The home pack was in complete ascendancy. Armitt and Bowden each scored tries as a result of clever runs, and Valentine, who made a try for Banks, later went over himself.

Cooper, who had started the season quietly by his standards, was much more his old self and scored four tries with the determination that was expected of him. Devery, who added seven goals, was also among the try scorers, the result of a pick-up, kick and follow-up.

Henderson and Rylance, who played one of his best games for Huddersfield, scored the Fartowners' other tries, Beck with a try and Buckle with a goal were the other points scorers for Rovers.

The following week, Huddersfield had to work hard to win their second round Yorkshire Cup game against York at Fartown. York played much better than the 19–7 score suggested. They positioned well and covered methodically so that the Huddersfield wings were given little room to move. In attack they backed up very well.

Banks kicked off and a burst down the middle by Cooper promised well, but it was all York in the first 15 minutes. Harker opened the scoring with a penalty after five minutes and, in spite of counterattacks in which Slevin and Rylance were prominent, York spent most of the time in Huddersfield territory. After 20 minutes Harker kicked a second goal. The Fartowners were now coming more into the picture, Cooper took them to York's '25'. Devery failed with a shot at goal, but shortly afterwards had another opportunity and was successful.

Huddersfield had established a position on the visitors' line and after a series of scrums Grace cut through to score by the posts; Devery added his second goal. Huddersfield went in at half-time 7–4 up.

After the break Large was hurt and had to leave the field before Cooper ran well down the touchline, unfortunately Hunter was unable to take his inside pass. After treatment Large returned and a further Huddersfield attack was rewarded with a penalty kicked by Devery. Huddersfield improved their lead in a move that began inside their own '25' where Bowden cut through a ruck and went on to near halfway where he passed to Valentine who finished an exciting race to the line with a try between the posts. Devery converted.

York's reply was to camp on the Fartowners' line and from a scrum in front of the posts Robinson broke to the left and after a 10-yard sprint passed inside for Harlow to score near the posts. Harker's kick at goal struck the upright and rebounded out. Ten minutes were left when Rylance snapped up a loose ball to dart over for another try. Devery improved it with a fine kick that gave him his fifth goal and meant that the Fartowners qualified for a semi-final place.

Two minutes from the end at Fartown on Wednesday 30 September, it seemed as if five goals by Devery would be good enough to put Huddersfield through to the Yorkshire Cup Final. But then Joe Phillips, Bradford Northern's full-back, kicked a goal to give the visitors an 11–10 victory.

Bradford won the toss and decided to have first half advantage of the strong wind. They used it to stay mainly in Huddersfield's half of the field. Bradford had most of the attacking play and after 14 minutes Phillips kicked a penalty before Trevor Foster broke loose from a tackle, drew the Fartown defence and passed to Hawes to score in the corner. Phillips added the extra points.

Huddersfield rallied strongly; Cooper almost went over in the corner, and then Brown went over the tryline, but knocked the flag down as he did so, and thus was deemed to be in touch. Then Northern were penalised at a scrum and Devery kicked the goal. A kick and follow-up by Cooper, who got his foot to a loose ball, tested the Bradford defence who held out to go in 7–2 up at half-time.

The second half was only 10 minutes old when Devery reduced the lead with a second goal, three minutes later he kicked a third as Bradford were penalised for offside. With the change of ends, Huddersfield, who had a slight superiority in the scrums in the first half, surprisingly failed to use the power of the wind. Cooper stole a loose ball and ran 40 yards but was stopped in his tracks with a great tackle by Storey.

The Fartowners camped on the Bradford line and when Goddard was penalised Devery landed his fourth goal, which gave Huddersfield the lead for the first time in the match.

They held it for seven minutes until they were penalised for offside in front of their own posts and Phillips put Northern a point ahead. About four minutes from the end, Devery won back the lead, but two minutes afterwards Huddersfield were offside from a scrum; Phillips landed his fourth goal and gave his side victory. The fluctuating score of the last 20 minutes made the issue exciting for the 15,438 crowd, but for Huddersfield it was so near – yet so far.

Huddersfield: J.C.H. Hunter, P. Henderson, G.R. Pepperell, P.C. Devery, L.W. Cooper, R. Rylance, W.M. Banks, E. Slevin, G. Curran, J. Bowden, J. Brown, C. Armitt, D.D. Valentine.
Bradford Northern: J. Phillips, R. Hawes, J. Mageen, W. Seddon, J. McLean, E. Jenkins, P. Goddard, B. Tyler, N. Haley, W. Jones, T. Foster, A. Storey, K. Traill.
Referee: T.W. Watkinson (Manchester)

Huddersfield's good league form continued after the Yorkshire Cup defeat. They won seven matches in a row, but after a couple of defeats at home to Bradford Northern and away to Wakefield Trinity, confidence was restored as Bradford Northern were beaten 11–8 at Odsal on 12 December. One match report said: "The principal factor in the Huddersfield victory was Lionel Cooper. They keep saying that Cooper is 'done' and that he isn't the power of old, but I doubt if the Bradford players subscribe to that view.

"The Australian's three tries were real match-winners, and the last two were reminiscent of his palmiest days in the manner in which he beat several defenders opposing him. Cooper scored all three tries, all of them the result of seizing promptly on what was at the start much less than half a chance and pursuing it with resolution.

"None was an easy try, none, in fact, ever looked like becoming a score until in the last split second it became clear it was, and many of us who saw his final try in the failing light from the other side of the field are likely to think that no Cooper try ever looked better. He had 40 yards to go and he covered the distance taking the shortest route, leaving behind him a trail of what appeared to be corpses."

After Christmas defeats home-and-away against Halifax, Huddersfield bounced back with home wins against Leeds, 34–0, and Featherstone Rovers, 21–18, before being drawn against Belle Vue Rangers to start their defence of the Challenge Cup.

The twice-postponed first round, first leg match at Belle Vue was played on Monday afternoon, 15 February 1954. There was, however, little sign of any cup tie enthusiasm – 15 minutes before the start the attendance was sparse – the postponement of the game had cost both clubs a great deal of money.

Huddersfield won the toss, Large took the ball from the kick-off, then Banks and Dyson opened out play, and a series of long-kicking exchanges were ended when Huddersfield invaded Rangers territory. A penalty against Huddersfield helped the home side get a footing inside the Fartowners' half, but after five minutes a kick by Banks and follow-up and tackle by Sullivan sent Rangers back, and Valentine, Bowden and Large opened out for Cooper to score in the corner. Devery missed the goalkick.

Rangers then staged two brief rallies with loose-forward Jennings going over for a try near the posts, Tierney converted. The lead was short-lived and from a play-the-ball from the middle of the field, Briggs received the ball from Valentine, broke through with ease and drew the full-back before passing to Large who scored under the posts, Devery had no difficulty in kicking the goal.

Devery and Tierney exchanged penalty goals to make the half-time score 10–7 to the Fartowners. In the second half Huddersfield added tries from Banks and Cooper and Devery added two goals. Belle Vue responded with scores from Day and Pugsley; Tierney kicked a goal. The Fartowners took a five-point advantage into the second leg two days later, having won 20–15.

Huddersfield, as they had in the first leg in Manchester, had Belle Vue on the back foot from the start. Large went over for a try after seven minutes play, Devery kicked the goal. Then Banks lost the ball but regained it and cut through before passing to Hunter who scored in the corner. It was too far out for Devery to convert.

Playing some good, hard rugby, Rangers replied with an

unconverted try from McGilvray, and when Huddersfield did get the ball Belle Vue's defensive marking made it hard for them to make any progress. The deadlock was broken, however, when Briggs seemed to have got over, but from the resultant scrum the ball was moved wide to Henderson who dived over at the corner for a try. Devery missed the kick.

Then, with half-time approaching, Briggs finished off a move after Henderson had burst down the middle. Devery kicked the goal – his 100th of the season – 98 for Huddersfield, two for Other Nationalities – so Huddersfield had built up a comfortable 16–6 interval lead.

The second half belonged to Huddersfield who ran in further tries from Briggs, Rylance, Cooper and Rose. Devery finished the game with five goals to make the final score 31–6. This set up another meeting between Huddersfield and St Helens, the previous season's finalists, in the second round at Fartown.

Before then, Doncaster, the babes of the League, visited Fartown in a league fixture on Saturday 20 February. The first half brought enough incident to satisfy everyone and after the first five minutes there was no doubt about the issue – Huddersfield were too clever and too fast for their opponents even though Doncaster had a good share of the attacking play.

The home side topped 50 in a scoring spree led by Cooper who ran in six tries, Henderson got a hat-trick, Rose with two, Devery and Briggs scored the others. Devery kicked seven goals with one from Rylance to make the final score 55–7.

However, it was a case of 'after the Lord Mayors Show' in their next fixture against Keighley at Lawkholme Lane because Huddersfield lost 7–5, which virtually put them out of the running for a top four position. This defeat, coupled with a 15–4 loss at Oldham, was disappointing.

At Oldham, Huddersfield had not much of the ball, at Keighley they had more than their share of possession but lacked ideas in attack – not a good omen with the cup tie against St Helens on the horizon.

The match at Fartown on Saturday 6 March 1954 was the most attractive of the second round Challenge Cup matches. By lunchtime, there was a crowd approaching 15,000, with long queues at the turnstiles. An hour before kick-off, the car park round the cricket field was practically filled. Many streets were also packed with cars. As trains from Lancashire arrived from noon onwards, St George's Square was continually busy with streams of people wearing the red and white St Helens colours.

Neither side, unfortunately, were quite at full strength. Huddersfield were without Banks, Saints were unable to play front-row forward Alan Prescott and Don Gullick, their Welsh international centre. Nonetheless, the teams were evenly matched and in the words of Jim Sullivan, the Saints coach, to the Huddersfield Football Committee, it seemed there would be "a reight good game".

From the kick-off, Huddersfield were penalised at the first play-the-ball, but Saints gained little ground with a kick to touch, before Rylance put Huddersfield inside the Saints half. From the scrum Dickinson broke away and kicked. Saints' winger Steve Llewellyn followed up and got his foot to the ball, but sent it dead. It was cut-and-thrust cup tie rugby. The Fartowners broke the deadlock when Bowden picked up a loose ball and fed Henderson who raced 30 yards to score. Devery missed the conversion.

After Huddersfield were penalised for handling in the scrum, Metcalfe reduced the arrears with a goal after 25 minutes. It was no-quarter-asked rugby, both defences held firm and the first half ended 3–2 to the Fartowners. Saints had had more of the attack, but Huddersfield's defence had been solid.

The second half started in the same way: Saints sustained a spell of possession, but after 10 minutes the home side increased their lead when Rylance fed Rose who went clean through to score. Devery added the goal points. With 25 minutes left Saints responded with a Llewellyn try, but when Huddersfield carried the ball into the Saints half, Devery kicked a penalty following a scrum offence. Huddersfield were now clearly on top and the Fartowners tackling was such that when Saints tried a passing move they lost almost 20 yards.

Saints made a last desperate attack, but try as he might, Ratcliffe could not get past Henderson; the final whistle signalled a hard-earned 12–5 win for Huddersfield.

Huddersfield: J.C.H. Hunter, P. Henderson, D. Rose, P.C. Devery, L.W. Cooper, R. Rylance, P. Bates, E. Slevin, H. Bradshaw, J. Bowden, J. Large, B. Briggs, D.D. Valentine.
St Helens: A.G. Moses, S. Llewellyn, D. Greenall, P. Metcalfe, Ratcliffe, J. Honey, J. Dickinson, Ayles, R. Blakemore, G. Parr, G. Parsons, W. Bretherton, R. Cale.
Attendance: 31,172

Huddersfield's Challenge Cup semi-final hopes were upset at Parkside in a third round tie with Hunslet on 20 March in front of a crowd of 20,136.

Alf Burnell kicked off and Huddersfield lost possession almost immediately. However, a knock-on by Hunslet brought a scrum and from this Bates broke away round the blindside to halfway, then Valentine found a gap before Rose and Henderson took the ball close to the line where Hunslet were penalised for offside. Devery opened the scoring with a penalty after five minutes.

Play returned to the Huddersfield '25' and from a scrummage Alf Burnell hoodwinked the defence and went through to score between the posts. Talbot converted. Good work by Gabbitas put Hunslet back in Fartown territory, the Parksiders were twice stopped inches short of the line, but a penalty brought Huddersfield breathing space before Briggs attacked, but could not get the ball away with Henderson well placed.

Back came Hunslet, with wingman Snowden stopped a few yards short of the corner. Hunslet won possession from the next scrum and Alf Burnell darted through in classic scrum-half style to score again by the posts, Talbot kicked the goal to put Hunslet eight points ahead five minutes before the interval. Just before half-time Devery narrowed the scores with a good goal but Hunslet went in 10–4 up at the break.

It had certainly been Hunslet's half, their tackling did not allow Huddersfield to get into their stride. Alf Burnell's cleverness near the line proved to be too much for the Fartowners to cope with. Hunslet again piled on the pressure in the second half, monopolised possession and gave the Huddersfield defence a torrid time.

Williamson soon scored in the corner, too far out for Talbot to convert. Huddersfield responded immediately with a try by Valentine just wide of the uprights, but surprisingly Devery missed the kick. Devery and Cooper rallied the Fartowners and took them upfield again, but Hunslet recovered possession and after a couple of play-the-balls Snowden wrapped up the game for Hunslet with a try in the corner to make it 16–7. The conversion failed, but even so, Huddersfield were out of the cup.

Hunslet: A. Talbot, A. Snowden, L. Williams, G. Waite, F. Williamson, B. Gabbitas, A. Burnell, D. Hatfield, Smith, W. Burnell, G. Gunney, E. Carroll, B. Shaw.

Huddersfield: J.C.H. Hunter, P. Henderson, D. Rose, P.C. Devery, L.W. Cooper, R. Rylance, P. Bates, E. Slevin, H. Bradshaw, J. Bowden, J. Large, P. Briggs, D.D. Valentine.

Referee: G.S. Phillips (Widnes)

It went from bad to worse. After the Hunslet defeat came an 11–3 reverse at Batley – this defeat was more inglorious than the cup exit –

and Huddersfield's chances of a top-four place had completely disappeared.

Sadly, the game at Mount Pleasant on 27 March 1954 was Pat Devery's last appearance in the claret and gold of Huddersfield – it seemed an ignominious end to an illustrious seven years at Fartown.

Huddersfield finished the season sixth in the league and were fourth in the Yorkshire League. However, it had been a disappointing campaign for their supporters in comparison to the previous season. The team had failed to make the top four and missed out on another Wembley appearance.

Devery kicked 116 goals for the season in all matches and both wingers, Cooper and Henderson, were once again well up in the national try scorers list with 40 and 32 respectively.

When the 1953–54 season finished, two retirements were announced by the Fartown club. The first was George Curran who played his final game for Huddersfield against Halifax at Thrum Hall on Boxing Day 1953, although he did not officially retire until 6 April 1954 when a hand injury sustained at work forced the end of his playing career. Although his stay at Fartown was comparatively brief, with 92 appearances and two tries, Curran did much good work in the forwards, particularly in the previous season's Challenge Cup run.

The second was the retirement of Pat Devery, which was announced on Easter Saturday 17 April 1954. It had been obvious for some time that he had been playing under a handicap and was unable to give 100 per cent to his game. The groin injury for which he had an operation during the 1950–51 season had finally taken its toll and terminated his career. He had played 223 games for Huddersfield, scored 98 tries and kicked 401 goals for a total of 1,096 points.

On 24 April 1954 'Autolycus' wrote in the *Huddersfield Daily Examiner* : "We shall be sorry not to see Devery on the field any more, but he has given us some imperishable memories – his display in a Championship semi-final at Wigan, and then the final at Maine Road against Warrington will not soon be forgotten. Then, too, there was a try scored at Leeds, when, like a dancing master, he flitted through a helpless opposition."

Stanley Chadwick in the *Rugby League Review* of 24 June 1954 wrote: "How successful a kicker was Devery? In each of the past two seasons he topped the century of goals, more interestingly perhaps are the following figures which show not only how many he kicked but also his number of misses. All the figures relate to Huddersfield club matches only. During season 1952–53, Devery kicked 142 goals from 303 attempts, in the season last ended (1953–54) he landed 114 from 212 attempts – I doubt if there are many players with a higher proportion of success over the last two campaigns.

Pat's last game in a Fartown jersey was at Batley when he captained the side that day, but it was a match in which things did not turn out too well for the 'claret and gold'. Rather would I take, as my last playing memory of him, the second round cup win against St Helens at Fartown on 6 March 1954... it was Huddersfield's best victory in a somewhat disappointing season.

The side played as a unit, each man doing the job allocated to him... Devery's task was to mark the danger man in the St Helens backs, Duggie Greenall, and he did it with such efficiency that the Saints captain was almost blotted out of the game.

Devery's smother tackle was, indeed, a deterrent to any opponent who found that he could neither run any further or pass the ball. Pat, as a player, was completely in the Fartown tradition... I do not ever remember seeing him earn an admonishment from the referee. His style of play was solely concerned with the best that can be got out of rugby league football.

His tackling, deadly and all-embracing though it was, was completely free from any trace of viciousness and in no phase of the game did he overstep the bounds of fair play.

Devery's retirement leaves a gap at Fartown. If the player who fills that gap can surpass the best that Pat Devery showed, then the club's supporters have some treats in store."

8. Lionel Cooper's finale

"Are there any new men coming?" was the question being asked by Huddersfield supporters at the beginning of the 1954–55 season. Where the new blood was to be found no-one was quite sure and much depended on whether the Australian ban was to be lifted in December.

At least 10 clubs, including Huddersfield, were genuinely looking to recruit players from Australia, so much so that they were not looking elsewhere – this was something of a gamble, for it was not certain that the Australians would allow English clubs to take the cream of their players.

In effect, the only Huddersfield signing prior to the start of the season was local prop forward David Flint, so the club had to rely on a similar playing staff to that at the end of the previous season, apart from the absence of Pat Devery. One player who claimed a regular place in the first team was Mick Sullivan, who took Devery's place at centre. Although very different in style to Devery, he scored fairly regularly and won a place in the Great Britain team that won the inaugural World Cup in France.

"Autolycus" in the *Huddersfield Examiner* wrote: "Still plenty of wing power…neither Henderson nor Cooper were quite the force last season they were the one before. The latter, who has been here nine years, is not as fast as he was. Twelve months ago he talked about giving up, we were happy that he did not and even though he is getting towards the veteran stage there is plenty of good football left in him. Henderson has plenty of tries in his bag and we must look forward to seeing him adding to the score in many a game yet.

"So long as both Hunter and Dyson are there we need have no fear for the full-back position."

Both Cooper and Henderson eased "Autolycus"'s fears in the opening match of the season. "Just like last season" was the verdict when Castleford were the visitors to Fartown on 14 August 1954.

After building up a lead and looking as though they were on top, Huddersfield slumped badly as Castleford went in 10–8 ahead at half-time. The Fartowners started the second half in grand style, Banks gained 30 yards with a kick to touch and from the scrum the ball came out to Huddersfield. Banks split the defence with a run down the middle before Rose fed Cooper who finished with a determined try in the corner.

It was all Huddersfield, very often it was Banks's prompting and probing that caused Castleford problems, but the biggest influence was stand-off Peter Ramsden who linked up with his centres at every opportunity. The result was four tries for Cooper and three for Henderson in a 43–17 triumph for the Fartowners. Rose, Sullivan and Ramsden also scored tries, Flint kicked three goals; Cooper and Hunter added one each.

It was more of the same the following week when Huddersfield travelled to Doncaster and came away with a 23–12 win. The score suggested that Huddersfield won comfortably, and in a sense they did, but not long before the end the Fartowners led only 18–12 and their lead was precarious.

Over long stretches of the game Huddersfield were clearly the better side. Doncaster, however, occasionally had the power to turn the tables, but Banks and Cooper had enough know-how to make the scoreline a respectable victory for the visitors. Once again, Huddersfield had moved the ball smartly with Banks the instigator of many attacking moves.

Banks scored two of Huddersfield's tries, Cooper got three – he would have had four, but the referee ruled that he bounced the ball over the line for the last one which was disallowed. Bradshaw was the other try scorer, Flint kicked three goals and Rylance got one.

A sunny, if windy, afternoon favoured Huddersfield for their Yorkshire Cup first round game with Keighley at Fartown on Saturday 11 September 1954.The opening exchanges were dominated by scrummages – there were three in the first two minutes before the ball came out on the Huddersfield side, the home side attacked on Cooper's flank.

A Keighley attack was stopped 30 yards from the line when they were penalised at the ensuing play-the-ball for Flint to open the scoring with a good goal after four minutes. The Fartowners, however, soon went further ahead. Cooper received the ball just inside Keighley territory and went on to beat two men, was checked three times by partial tackles, but finished with a characteristic try wide out. Flint's shot at goal hit a post and bounced the wrong side for the Fartowners.

Keighley won possession, made good use of the ball and gradually worked their way back up the field where Hollindrake was held just short of the Fartown line. Valentine and Henderson led the way back to the visitors '25' where Huddersfield opened out to the left, Sullivan made a neat burst before offloading to Cooper who scored by the posts. Flint kicked the goal.

Huddersfield C & AC Supporters Club presentation, 1954.
Mr. E. Starkey (right), President of the Supporters Club, presents Pat Devery (left) with an illuminated address – a special tribute including words and a picture – for services to Huddersfield rugby league prior to his impending return to Australia in August 1954, watched by Mr. S. Garside (Huddersfield Hospitals Broadcast commentator). (Courtesy *Huddersfield Examiner*)

October 1954. Lionel Cooper admires the statuette he received from the Huddersfield C & AC Supporters Club, for breaking Albert Rosenfeld's club record 366 tries. Rosenfeld is on the left, Jim Bowden looks on.
(Courtesy *Huddersfield Examiner*)

Keighley rallied, but Valentine tore a hole in the defence before he threw a long pass to Banks who fed Henderson for a try; Flint again converted. Undismayed, Keighley continued to attack, but a pass to Hollindrake missed the mark. Back came Huddersfield, Cooper picked up the ball on his own '25', handed off two opponents before he grounded the ball to score his third try of the afternoon, again Flint kicked the goal.

Keighley went forward yet again, Baines made a good opening for Hallas to score a try wide out, but Lockwood failed with the conversion. A minute later, Flint increased Huddersfield's lead with a good penalty goal.

It was all Huddersfield for the next 10 minutes or so as Valentine and Banks dictated play. When Keighley were penalised for encroaching offside, Flint was successful with the penalty to make the half-time score 24–3 to Huddersfield.

Keighley had not looked 20 points worse than Huddersfield. They had had a good share of possession and looked dangerous, but Huddersfield's breakaways had been devastating with Cooper hard to stop.

The restart saw Keighley on the attack and passing by Woosey saw Brown score by the posts, surprisingly Lockwood failed with the kick. A run by Cooper put Huddersfield on the attack, but he was pushed into touch on the Keighley'25'. Then a neat burst by Sullivan took the Fartowners to the Keighley line, the ball was flipped back to Valentine and he crashed over for a try which Flint converted.

After some strenuous work just inside the Huddersfield half, Valentine burst through and handed onto Henderson who finished with a clever run-in. Flint added the goal points. Keighley were not done and their determination was rewarded when Banks completely missed the ball when it was heeled out of a scrum near the line – Brown snapped it up to go over for try which Hollindrake converted.

Huddersfield were stung into action; Cooper raced through the Keighley defence down the middle of the field to score the Fartowners' seventh try. Flint's kick hit the outside of the upright.

Keighley refused to give up and spread-eagled the Huddersfield defence with some great passing for Brown to score the visitors' fourth try of the afternoon; the goal kick by Hollindrake failed.

Still Keighley kept it up, and when Sullivan dropped a pass Hollindrake picked up the ball to score under the posts. Hallas unfortunately failed to convert. Virtually on the stroke of time, Cooper scored a further unconverted try, his fifth, for Huddersfield to make the final score 40–17. Keighley's enterprise had made for an entertaining cup tie in front of 10,572 fans – Huddersfield's biggest gate of the season so far.

Cooper had been in great form. One report said: "Cooper's powerful shoulders and hips can still brush opponents aside with ease and the telling hand-off has lost little if any of its power. While he has never been acclaimed as a speed merchant, he has even this season run in tries from halfway with opponents trying to catch him from behind."

The teams that day were:
Huddersfield: J.C.H. Hunter, P. Henderson, D. Rose, M. Sullivan, L.W. Cooper, P. Ramsden, W.M. Banks, E. Slevin, Wood, D. Flint, J. Fairbank, P. Briggs, D.D. Valentine.
Keighley: Lockwood, T. Hollindrake, Holgate, D. Hallas, Redman, E. Verrenkamp, Brown, Woosey, Traill, Raines, Murphy, Bell, Holdbrook.
Referee: C.F. Appleton (Warrington)

Featherstone Rovers provided Huddersfield with some stiff opposition the following week at Fartown, but the strong running of Henderson, who scored one try, and Cooper, who got three, provided an attack that had a variety of resources for which Rovers had no answer. Huddersfield ran out winners 23–14.

Hull visited Fartown in the second round of the Yorkshire Cup on Tuesday 21 September and confidence was high after the comprehensive victory against Keighley in the first round. The match was played in atrocious conditions – there was a gale blowing diagonally along the pitch and the rain beat down with a fierce intensity that must have chilled the players to the bone and perhaps, on the whole, a 7–7 draw was a fair result.

Huddersfield had to face the weather at kick-off and they had long spells on the defensive with either Francis or Turner driving them back with kicks whenever they tried to gain good ground. After 25 minutes Hutton put Hull ahead with a penalty, but almost immediately the Fartowners responded with a great individual try by Sullivan, who got the ball on halfway, broke a tackle, kicked ahead and won the race with Hutton to gather and score. Flint kicked the goal to put Huddersfield three points in front.

But not for long – five minutes before half-time Huddersfield were on the attack, but dropped the ball, Francis picked up and with Watts in support kicked ahead. The Hull winger streaked after the ball which bounced up nicely for him on the line enabling him to score under the posts. Hutton converted to put Hull 7–5 up at the break.

With a slender lead and having to face the wind and the rain, Hull's position did not look promising, but 10 minutes slipped by, then 15, then 20, but still they held the lead until eventually they were penalised in front of the posts and Flint levelled the scores.

Huddersfield had failed to make full use of the conditions – Flint had two more chances before the end with penalties from near halfway, but by then the ball was wet and heavy and neither kick had height or direction. Both teams resigned themselves to a replay at The Boulevard two days later on Thursday 23 September.

Despite a first minute try by Cooper which equalled Rosenfeld's career try scoring record for the club, Huddersfield were knocked out of the Yorkshire Cup 22–13."The Scout" in the *Huddersfield Examiner* reported: "Hull's forwards were the complete masters of the Huddersfield six, for not only could they keep the Huddersfield men bunched together, but when the ball went out they could move across field smartly and there was never any mistake in their tackling...the Hull pack used the last 10 minutes of the game for practice moves."

The teams for The Boulevard encounter were:
Hull: C. Hutton, W. Riches, C.R. Turner, R.L. Francis, I. Watts, B. Conway, A. Tripp, M. Scott, T. Harris, R. Coverdale, H. Markham, N. Hockley, A. Bedford.
Scorers: Tries: Riches, Watts, Markham, Conway. Goals: Hutton 5.
Huddersfield: J.C.H. Hunter, P. Henderson, D. Rose, M. Sullivan, L.W. Cooper, R. Rylance, W.M. Banks, E. Slevin, H. Bradshaw, D. Flint, J. Fairbank, J. Bowden, D.D. Valentine.
Scorers: Tries: Sullivan, Cooper, Rylance. Goals: Flint 2.

There was a significant game at Fartown on Saturday 2 October 1954 when Hunslet were beaten 30–16 in a game when the score did not exaggerate the supremacy of the home side. Both sides played fast open rugby and succeeded in making play for their wingers, which ensured a minimum of tedious play-the-balls gave the 11,316 spectators a good 80 minutes of attacking rugby.

From the outset there was pressure on the home line when a dropped pass was pounced on by Waite to score a try goaled by Geoff Gunney. Huddersfield's reply was not long delayed – it was left to Lionel Cooper to pull the game round in his team's favour with one of his non-stop tries.

He opened Huddersfield's scoring after 15 minutes to the obvious delight of his colleagues and the crowd alike, because his touchdown set a record total of tries for the Huddersfield club. It beat Rosenfeld's try aggregate of 366.

96

Cooper had three tries in all to match those of forward Brian Briggs, in what had been a hard, fast and exciting game.

Huddersfield: J.C.H. Hunter, P. Henderson, P. Ramsden, M. Sullivan, L.W. Cooper, R. Rylance, P. Bates, E. Slevin, H. Bradshaw, J. Bowden, J. Large, B. Briggs, D.D. Valentine.

Scorers: Tries: Cooper 3, Briggs 3, Sullivan, Valentine. Goals: Rylance 3.

Hunslet: E. Backhouse, J. Evans, L. Williams, G. Waite, F. Williamson, R. Williams, A. Talbot, D. Hatfield, F. Smith, W. Burnell, G. Gunney, E. Carroll, G. James.

Scorers: Tries: L. Williams, Waite. Goals: Gunney 5.

Two weeks later, on Thursday 21 October, Albert Rosenfeld himself made a presentation of a statuette to Cooper on behalf of Huddersfield Supporters Club to commemorate the feat of beating 'Rozzy's' own try scoring record.

Cooper told the packed audience that he had enjoyed every minute of his stay in Huddersfield since he came in 1947: "When I came at first I never ceased to hear of the great players of the past, but this continual ramming home of the names of the palmy days, Wagstaff, Clark, Gronow, Gleeson and, of course, Rozzy, serves to create a grand tradition and gives you something to live up to. Perhaps in years to come a future generation of supporters will speak of the 1948, 1949 and 1950 team in a similar strain."

A.N. Gaulton, on behalf of the Supporters Club, added: "We have been fortunate in having the services of such men [Rosenfeld and Cooper] at widely different periods. The game has been better for their presence, and their standard remains a consistently high one. Wing power at Fartown has always been the envy of many clubs and it is a tribute to these two Australians that among a galaxy of stars they stand out."

Fartown supporters did not have long to wait before Cooper again showed his try-scoring prowess. When Wakefield Trinity were the visitors to Fartown on Saturday 27 November, Cooper's strong finishing played a great part in a 25–8 win.

He scored five tries in all and a press report in Cooper's testimonial booklet *Lionel* said: "Whether Cooper, Bevan or Rosenfeld is the greatest winger is a matter for an argument that could be debated a long time. The other two wings have (or have had) their own 'specials', but some of these scored by Cooper on Saturday against Wakefield could have been accomplished by neither of the other two."

As in the Yorkshire Cup earlier in the season, Huddersfield made an early exit from the Challenge Cup. In a game which was touch and go to the last minute when Huddersfield, in front of the Leeds posts, might have snatched a draw, the home side at Headingley on Saturday 12 February 1955, put paid to Huddersfield's hopes by beating them 8–3.

There was nothing to choose between the sides after the first half, and when Henderson scored in the corner in the second half after Large and Ramsden handled, it seemed as though Huddersfield had the measure of their opponents.

The Leeds defence had been tight and left no gaps and for the first time had been stretched to breaking point, but the Fartowners found themselves on their own line and were caught napping and, although a penalty goal by Jones was the only result, Leeds won a great advantage in morale.

Huddersfield piled on the pressure, following which Cooper decided to take a long range kick at goal from a penalty, but the kick fell short. From this Leeds regained possession and ran the ball out to the left where the movement finished with a try from Scholes.

It was a blow to the Fartowners, particularly after Henderson had earlier knocked on a foot from the Leeds line trying to pick up the ball at pace. It was not going to be Huddersfield's day; especially after many of their supporters claimed the first Leeds try from Turnbull came from a forward pass.

Even though Ramsden had two or three good runs and Hunter came near to scoring in the last few minutes it was not to be. Huddersfield were out of the cup.

Leeds: J. Dunn, A. Turnbull, K.A. McLellan, B. L. Jones, D. Scholes, G. Brown, J. Stevenson, A. Skelton, A. Wood, W.E. Hopper, B. Poole, W. Hanson, C. Last.
Scorers: Tries: Turnbull, Scholes. Goal: Jones.
Huddersfield: F. Dyson, P. Henderson, G. Roughley, J.C.H. Hunter, L.W. Cooper, P. Ramsden, W.M. Banks, E. Slevin, H. Bradshaw, J. Bowden, J. Large, W. Griffin, D.D. Valentine.
Scorer: Try: Henderson.
Referee: C.F. Appleton (Warrington)
Attendance: 21,791

Huddersfield, in their first home game since the end of January 1955, entertained Batley on Saturday 12 March. Oddly enough, until their second-rower Payne was sent off for his tackle on Valentine, Batley had hardly ever looked able to extend their opponents who had far more moves and were quicker and stronger, reflected in a score of 41–10.

Huddersfield should have put more points on the board, the reason why they did not was that only four goals were added to the 11 tries they scored. Dyson's lengthy kicks to touch gained the Fartowners good ground, with Hunter's running always a danger to the Batley defence. Cooper added three more tries to his tally, Henderson and Roughley scored twice, and a try each went to Large, Rylance, Ramsden and Bowden. Dyson kicked three goals and Cooper one.

Conditions were poor at Mount Pleasant a week later when Huddersfield played the return with Batley. It was raining hard at kick-off and the playing area was in parts waterlogged. Indeed, the referee, Eric Clay, was justified in stopping the game at least 10 minutes early because by then he could not distinguish one side from the other.

The decision would not have been unfair to Batley for Huddersfield were well on top, leading 21–0. Both sides had tried to open out play and in the circumstances this was remarkable, but it was not surprising that promising moves were often checked by the difficulty of controlling the ball. The Huddersfield forwards played well together as a unit and behind them Ramsden and Rylance varied moves with neat grubber kicks on the ground, while Hunter's straight running and Dyson's fielding and kicking stood out. Again, as in the game with Batley at Fartown, Cooper scored three tries, Rylance and Hunter added one each. Rylance kicked two goals and Dyson one.

Further Cooper try hat-tricks came against Workington Town at Fartown in a 44–13 win, when Henderson scored four tries, and at Crown Flatt against Dewsbury when Huddersfield won 42–0.

As it turned out, the significance of Huddersfield's final league game of the season at Borough Park against Workington Town on Saturday 7 May 1955 was Lionel Cooper's final appearance in claret and gold.

In many ways it was a typical end-of the-season affair. Workington won 33–8. Huddersfield's passing and handling left a lot to be desired, particularly once when they were attacking near the line only to give the ball away for Workington to go the length of the field for a try. More tries were stopped by Johnny Hunter's last ditch tackles.

Workington Town: S. Thompson, I. Southward, A. Paskins, E. Gibson, J. Vickers, K. Faulder, J. Roper, J. Hayton, W. Lymer, A. Key, J. Mudge, B. Edgar, W. Ivison.
Scorers: Tries: Southward 2, Gibson 2, Paskins, Vickers, Mudge. Goals: Thompson 5, Gibson.
Huddersfield: J.C.H. Hunter, N. Wainwright, G. Roughley, M. Sullivan, L.W. Cooper, W.M. Banks, P. Ramsden, E. Slevin, H. Bradshaw, J. Bowden, B. Briggs, J. Large, D.D. Valentine.
Scorers: Tries: Cooper, Ramsden. Goal: Bowden.

On the whole, it had been a disappointing season at Fartown, the poorest of any since the war. Huddersfield failed to win a single trophy, not even the Charity Cup. The Fartowners had been the best attacking combination in the league, but still finished in 11th place because their defensive qualities let them down. Their points tally was helped greatly by the scoring ability of Cooper and Henderson.

Cooper finished top of the national try-scoring list with 66, Henderson third with 45 – these two, plus Brian Bevan, were a trio of wingmen who stood head and shoulders above the rest. Contrary to pre-season expectations, Cooper had one of his best seasons and took his try aggregate beyond the 400 mark.

On reflection, it was a season which opened promisingly and ended, except for the final match, very well, but faded in the middle. Between 18 December, when they played Leigh at home, and 5 March, a trip to York, the Fartowners played nine matches and won only two. One of the defeats was against Leeds in the Challenge Cup, but the six league defeats – five at Fartown – put them out of the running for the top four play-off places.

Huddersfield and Hunslet players took part in two end-of-the-season testimonial matches for Lionel Cooper, at Fartown, and Ted Carroll, at Hunslet. In the encounter at Fartown on Monday 9 May 1955, no fewer than 18 tries were scored, so the 3,427 crowd could justifiably claim to have had their money's worth. Huddersfield scored 11of them and Hunslet seven, as each side kicked five goals the Fartowners ended winners 43–31.

With Henderson injured, Huddersfield brought in Billy Boston, Wigan's international winger as a guest player. He was the star of the match, scored five tries and showed a clever judgement of pace coupled with a sidestep that was devastating. Naturally, in games such as these, the emphasis is on attack, the tackling and covering are fairly secondary.

The *Huddersfield Examiner* said: "Cooper was given no latitude, Boston fully earned his tries and towards the end there was some barging incidents that suggested that the players had their hearts fully in the game... on the whole it was a bright game that gave the season a pleasant ending." Boston, with five, Rylance, who got two, Cooper, Banks, Pepperell and Ramsden were the Huddersfield try scorers. Rylance, Griffin, Ramsden, Pepperell and Banks kicked the goals.

James, with a hat-trick, Gapper, Shaw, Williams and Gunney scored tries for Hunslet and Talbot kicked five goals.

Huddersfield: Pepperell, Boston (Wigan), Roughley, Rylance, Cooper (c), Banks, Ramsden, Slevin, Wood, Flint, Briggs, Griffin, Large.

Hunslet: Evans, Gunney, James, Harrison, Carroll, R Williams (c), Talbot, Hatfield, Smith, Gapper (Huddersfield), Clues, Shaw, Traill (Bradford N).

Referee: Tom Armitage (Huddersfield)

In the corresponding game at Parkside on Wednesday 11 May, there was an experiment with a new play-the-ball rule. The proposed new rule saw a team tackled twice consecutively handing over the ball to the other side and it worked quite well when tried in the second half.

The idea was to eliminate players 'dying' with the ball, and to bring back the almost-forgotten art of kicking. The players seemed to adapt well with the rule and it was noticeable that the second half produced more open play.

Both Huddersfield and Hunslet turned out scratch sides, with the game being played in a light-hearted manner. It was fitting that Carroll should score a try, although Whittaker turned a blind eye when he broke through.

Cooper paced himself nonchalantly through the game, but showed glimpses of his class and power with three tries as the Fartowners eased their way to a 28–13 victory.

The other try scorers for Huddersfield were Goodyear, Griffin, Lindley, Bates and Wood. Cooper and Briggs kicked one goal each. Shaw and Clues scored Hunslet's other tries, Evans added two goals.

Hunslet: Evans, Gunney, R. Williams, Langton, Williamson, Gabbitas, Slater, Hatfield, Gapper, Shaw, Carroll, Clues, James.

Huddersfield: Whittaker, Lees, Valentine, Large, Cooper, Pepperell, Bates, Goodyear, Wood, Lindley (Wakefield T), Griffin, Fairbank, Briggs.

Huddersfield 43 Hunslet 31, Lionel Cooper testimonial match at Fartown, 9 May 1955. Cooper touches down, watched by: Ron Rylance, Russ Pepperell, Jack Large and Peter Ramsden (Huddersfield). Ken Traill, back in the colours of his old club, looks on.

9. Hunter completes 10 years

One of the last things Johnny Hunter could have expected when he came to England was that he would eventually be the successor to Lionel Cooper on the left wing in the Fartown team, but this was the case in 1955–56. Lionel's retirement and the emergence of new full-back Frank Dyson gave Hunter the difficult job of replacing Cooper which he undertook in his own inimitable style.

At the same time, Hunter was ever ready with a word of advice, encouragement and – when needed – criticism of the young Dyson who succeeded him at full-back.

In retrospect, season 1955–56 was one of frequent disappointments for Fartowners, and although there were times when the team raised hopes that the long overdue revival was on its way, the promise was never fulfilled.

Huddersfield's position in the final league table was very moderate by Fartown standards, and they came to an early end in the Yorkshire Cup when they were well beaten in the first round at Featherstone. There was some progress in the Challenge Cup but they were comprehensively beaten at Wigan in the third round 24–2.

The results of the first few league matches made pretty good reading, despite a defeat in the first game at Rochdale. Huddersfield rattled up good scores at Fartown against Castleford, 30–6, Keighley, 48–14 and Bramley, 46–7, as well as a 36–9 win at Batley.

However, a 38–11 defeat at Leigh was the start of six consecutive league defeats and, apart from victories against New Zealand and York at Fartown and a well-earned 18–14 win at Headingley against Leeds, there was little to enthuse over before the end of the year with Huddersfield 23rd in the table.

The Fartowners' form was, to say the least, erratic in the New Year – there was encouragement with Challenge Cup wins over Whitehaven and Swinton, but the improvement was not maintained.

The team did, however, rise a few places in the table to finish in 14th position, and with more victories than defeats. It was commonly felt before the season started that Lionel Cooper was going to be greatly missed and the left wing position would reveal a weakness.

Cooper was missed, but Hunter and Sullivan, who in the main shared the position, were more than up to the task. Hunter, who was granted a testimonial, brought his usual unorthodoxy to good effect, and ended the season with 13 tries. Sullivan, although he missed many games through international and county commitments, finished top scorer with 26 tries.

Dyson topped the century of goals, with 106 for the season and also won county honours.

In a way, the 1956–57 season was the end of an era in Huddersfield's history. Three players retired at the end of it – Jim Bowden, Bill Griffin and Johnny Hunter.

After looking early in the season as though they were capable of securing a place in the top four, Huddersfield produced some substandard displays which left them in ninth place in the final league table. Following a 41–2 first round Yorkshire Cup win at Fartown over Batley, the Fartowners went out of the competition at Belle Vue against Wakefield Trinity, narrowly losing 13–11 but, by the end of October, Huddersfield were almost unbelievably in the top four with practically the same team which had so often proved disappointing the previous season.

The way in which the 1955–56 champions Hull, 26–5, and Leeds, 26–12, were beaten at Fartown gave their supporters further confidence.

As events proved, Huddersfield fell off the pace as home defeats at the hands of Batley, 13–9, Keighley, 10–7, Halifax, 17–13 and Hull KR 13–10, proved bad for morale on and off the field. After drawing 5–5 at Swinton in the first round of the Challenge Cup, Huddersfield won the replay 5–0 at Fartown but, after winning 6–2 at Salford, went out in the third round losing 10–0 at Barrow, the eventual Wembley finalists.

Ironically, after a further four consecutive home defeats, the Fartowners made amends with well-deserved wins at Wigan, 13–8, Bradford, 26–7, Barrow, 21–13 and Featherstone 26–18.

On the individual front, Mick Sullivan maintained his fine international record by playing in all three tests against Australia and all three games against France. He was the only Fartowner to be selected in the 1957 World Cup squad.

For Frank Dyson it looked, at one time, like being a goalkicking record season. His century before Christmas opened up visions of establishing new club and league figures. Unfortunately his accuracy deserted him and his final figure of 141 did not fulfil expectations.

Johnny Hunter, once again, played most of his rugby at centre or on the wing, with the Warrington game at Fartown on 13 April 1957 an unfortunate choice for his last match in Fartown's colours.

Johnny Hunter's last gesture to the Fartown crowd.
Johnny strips off his jersey and throws it into the crowd at the end of his last game for Huddersfield, against Warrington on 13 April 1957.

With Hunter showing his skills and daring at full-back, Huddersfield were a well-beaten side on the day losing 28–8 – Hunter stripped off his jersey at the end and threw it into the crowd as a last gesture to the Fartown supporters. He had racked up 332 games for Huddersfield, scored 74 tries and kicked three goals.

Hunter wasn't exactly idle in the summer months either. A natural ball-player, he excelled at golf, tennis and cricket –as well as being a forceful batsman, he was well above average as a wicketkeeper.

For the summer of 1947, he had joined Bradley Mills Cricket Club who played in the Huddersfield and District League. Club cricket was a serious matter in the north of England. Many clubs employed a professional player, often from an international background. Big crowds would come to the matches. On Saturday 31 May, Bradley Mills played a first round Sykes Cup match against Kirkburton.

Unfinished on the Saturday, the game was carried over to the following Monday evening and Bradley Mills totalled 488 all out. Hunter contributed 178, the *Huddersfield Examiner* reported: "His innings was featured by some hurricane hitting, all clean, full-bloodied hits and crisp drives."

Alec Lodge, a past president and stalwart of the Huddersfield League, writing in the *Drakes Huddersfield Cricket League Centenary Brochure 1881–1981* said: "Hunter's cricket was as exhilarating as his football."

In reply, Kirkburton made 254 in a match during which 742 runs

105

were scored in fewer than 10 hours, amazing in those days of unlimited time cup ties. As happens in life, in the second round, Hunter failed to trouble the scorers.

Bradley Mills were not a good side and finished bottom of Section B, but might be unique because as well as having the highest score of 488 of the season they also had the lowest – 32 all out against Almondbury on 17 May.

Hunter also had spells with Salts in the Bradford League and Rochdale in the Lancashire League. His final four seasons were with Lightcliffe in the Bradford League, from 1953 to 1956. In 1955 they won the Bradford League's Priestley Cup.

Jim Holroyd, who was a professional opening bowler during Johnny's four seasons with the club, recalls: "Hunter was one of the best cover points I've seen. He took a great catch off my bowling when we played against East Bierley. Harry Waterhouse, who was a Yorkshire Colt and notorious hard driver of the ball, drove me into the covers. The ball didn't go six inches off the ground and was really travelling when Johnny flung himself to his right and took it one-handed ...that wicket was a real feather in my cap.

In the 1955 cup semi-final, Johnny was not out 40-something overnight and very nervous before play the following evening. He got his 50, but was out soon afterwards, however, his runs won us a tight game. He liked pickled onions... I've seen him sit down and eat a whole jar in the tea interval, and liked his three or four pints. He took over a post office when he returned to Australia, and I heard he put on a lot of weight."

Don Garside, who was Lightclffe's wicketkeeper in 1955 and 1956, recalls: "He was a nice fellow... easy going. I remember him dancing on the table in the Sun Inn in his striped underpants after we'd won the cup against Pudsey St Lawrence at Park Avenue, Bradford, Bank Holiday Monday, 1955. Johnny scored 0 in the final." Johnny wore glasses when he played cricket, and his eyesight wasn't all that good without them. Donald Garside once asked him how he went on under a high ball when he was playing rugby: "I can't see the ball; I just guess," he replied. Garside remembers: "He used to field at cover point — threw in underhand, but had a strong throw. People came to watch Lightcliffe because they admired Johnny as a rugby player.

Cyril Pickard, who was first team opening bat during Johnny's time at Lightcliffe, remembers: "He was an aggressive batsman... fearless Aussie... bit of a lad... full of beans... very friendly... a brilliant fielder, he could scamper like nobody. When he was fielding he used to try and spot someone in the crowd with a radio so that he could keep up-to-date with the racing results. When we batted second, I hadn't time to eat my sandwich before we went out. More than once, when I came back, Johnny had scoffed it."

John Barritt, who played occasionally for the first team, but more in the seconds; and was there for all four years Johnny played at the club remembers him as a: 'Big-hitter batting at four or five; he'd get you a quick 50 or a quick none. Flamboyant ... did everything in a wild and wonderful way ... well-liked ... Not a named professional I don't think."

Keith Hirst, who was a young man at the time, and occasional first-team player recalls: "Grand chap ... so much enthusiasm. When we practised he could give us catching practice by hitting the ball straight up in the air, so high that you almost lost sight of it before it started coming down."

In 1953 he made 400 runs at an average of 36.36 and was top of the club's batting averages. In 1954 he scored 378 runs at 23.62 and was second in the averages. He kept wicket for most of the season because Roy Booth was away playing for Yorkshire; Booth only played three games for Lightcliffe in 1954. In 1955 Hunter made 443 runs at 27.68; and was third in the averages. In 1956, his final season, he scored 301 runs at 23.15; and was second in the averages.

On his return to Australia in 1957, he joined the Port Kembla Cricket Club and for a short time played as a wicketkeeper. He had a long period of absence from the sport but decided to end a 10-year retirement after watching the young Port Kembla team at the end of the 1966–67 season.

Swayed by the fact that their experienced captain was leaving, at the age of 42, Hunter took over the captaincy at the beginning of the 1967–68 season and also became the regular wicketkeeper. He drew on his experience to inspire his youthful team and they won both the Minor Premiership and Major Premiership for Port Kembla for the first time in 23 years, and the following season, 1968–69, again with Hunter in charge, retained the Minor Premiership.

In 1969–70, his last season, Hunter led Port Kembla into the final after they had to win their last three matches to make the semi-finals. However, they were beaten in a close contest by Corrimal.

Then, after three seasons with Port Kembla as their captain, Hunter announced his final retirement from cricket and returned to his next sporting challenge – golf.

International rugby league stars playing cricket. Back: Ernest Ward, Johnny Hunter, Lionel Cooper, Arthur Clues and Barry Tyler. Front: Bert Cook seems to be enjoying his job of nursing Johnny Hunter's son Glenn.

He had joined Port Kembla Golf Club in 1957 and was an active member right up to 1980. Among various roles in the club, Hunter served as a director in 1972 and 1973. He played several years as a representative for the club in both the White Horse Cup and 'B' Pennant competitions. Nothing seemed to elude Hunter, and he achieved what every golfer dreams of – a hole in one on the 12th hole at the Port Kembla course.

10. International recognition

As well as playing for Huddersfield, the Fartown Aussies achieved international recognition, mainly in the Other Nationalities side, but also in various other representative matches.

In May 1949, Hunter, Cooper and Devery were included in a British Empire squad for a two match tour of France. The tour party included strong contingents from Huddersfield and Workington Town. In the first game against France at Bordeaux on Thursday 26 May, Hunter was at full-back, but left the field due to a sprained shoulder, shortly followed by Mudge, the Australian second-row forward, who was also injured. The handicap was too much for the touring side who were beaten 23–10. The Empire team took on a Pyrenees XIII at Albi on Sunday 29 May in the second game – Devery scored a hat-trick of tries, Cooper also added a try in a 38–12 win.

Tour Party

	A	T	G	Pts
W.M. Banks (Huddersfield)	2	0	0	0
A.H. Bath (Warrington)	2	2	0	6
R. Bartlett (Leeds)	2	0	0	0
H.E. Cook (Leeds)	1	0	7	14
L.W. Cooper Huddersfield)	2	2	0	6
J.C. Daly (Huddersfield)	2	0	0	0
P.C. Devery (Huddersfield)	2	3	2	13
J.C.H. Hunter (Huddersfield)	1	0	0	0
W. Ivison (Workington T)	1	0	0	0
V. McKeating (Workington T)	2	0	0	0
R. McMaster (Leeds)	2	0	0	0
J. Mudge (Workington T)	1	0	0	0
A.H. Paskins (Workington T)	2	2	0	6
G.R. Pepperell (Huddersfield)	2	0	0	0
D.D. Valentine (Huddersfield)	2	1	0	3

Meanwhile, international rugby league in post-war Europe was at its height in the years between 1949 and 1955. September 1949 saw the introduction of a European championship which featured England, France and Wales, as well as the reincarnation of an Other Nationalities team. Other Nationalities was originally conceived in 1904, to provide the new sport with international matches, and lasted until 1906. It was formed again in 1921 and lasted until 1933.The side was composed of players who did not qualify for the three other countries.

Fartown 3 December 1949. Presentation of Other Nationalities international caps, before the match against Salford, by Mr. J. Wood-Beever (Huddersfield chairman) to Lionel Cooper, Dave Valentine and Pat Devery.
(Courtesy *Huddersfield Examiner*)

Initially made up with players of Scottish and Welsh origin in 1904, the growth in the number of players from other countries, particularly Australia and New Zealand, who came to play in English rugby league following the Second World War, made it potentially a very strong side.

Overseas players to wear the distinctive emerald green jersey included Fartown's Australian trio of Johnny Hunter, Lionel Cooper and Pat Devery, New Zealander Peter Henderson and Scottish loose-forward Dave Valentine and the Irish prop John Daly.

Others who played for Other Nationalities included Warrington's Harry Bath and Brian Bevan, the irrepressible Arthur Clues of Leeds, along with Workington Town's Australians Tony Paskins and Johnny Mudge. Players such as Dave Valentine could also play for Great Britain, but for Australians and New Zealanders who were based in England, these matches were their only chance of international competitive action. Some had played for their home country before coming to England, but for many great players, including Brian Bevan, Harry Bath and Ces Mountford, these matches were their only international appearances.

The first match under the new International Championship format was against England at Borough Park, Workington, on 19 September

1949. Despite a 6pm kick-off, a crowd of 17, 576 was present.

The Other Nationalities side had 10 Australians in their line-up, including Lionel Cooper and Pat Devery, who captained the side and kicked a goal in a 13–7 win. Also in the side were Huddersfield's Scottish winger George Wilson, who played at full-back and scored a try, with fellow Scot Dave Valentine at loose-forward.

Hunter made his Other Nationalities debut in a 6–5 win against Wales at The Park, Abertillery, on 22 October. Bevan and Cooper scored the tries in a game played in heavy icy rain in front of only 2,000. The captains asked the referee, Charlie Appleton, to cut the game short, but he refused. Pat Devery had moved to play at centre, Ces Mountford took the stand-off position.

Other Nationalities' final match was on 15 January 1950 against France in Marseilles. Hunter and Devery were part of a five-strong Huddersfield contingent, but France won 8–3 in front of 20,000 fans. Both England and Other Nationalities had won two of their matches, but England took the title through a superior points difference.

1949–50 Championship table:

	P	W	D	L	Pts	F	A
England	3	2	0	1	4	31	24
Other Nationalities	3	2	0	1	4	22	20
Wales	3	1	0	2	2	27	25
France	3	1	0	2	2	21	32

Lionel Cooper was the only one of the Fartown Australians to play in the first two Other Nationalities matches in the 1950-51 European Championship. The first match was against France in Bordeaux, and the home side won 16-3. On 31 March, only 5,000 supporters saw a high-scoring match in Swansea, when Other Nationalities beat Wales 27-21. Cooper was one of seven try scorers for his side; Peter Henderson and Dave Valentine were the other two Huddersfield players in the team.

Other Nationalities included Hunter, Devery, Cooper, Daly and Valentine when they completed their fixtures against England at Central Park, Wigan, on 11 April 1951.

Devery kicked five goals, and Daly and Valentine scored a try each in a resounding 35–10 win – which equalled their biggest-ever score of 35–19 against England in 1930 – but because France beat Wales 28–13 in Marseilles four days later the championship eluded them, and they finished as runners-up again due to on an inferior points difference.

111

Other Nationalities 35 England 10, 11 April 1951. Players: Back: Brian Bevan (Warrington), John Mudge (Workington T), John Daly (Huddersfield), Bob Robson (Salford), Tom McKinney (Salford), Trevor Allan (Leigh), Johnny Hunter (Huddersfield); front: Pat Devery (Huddersfield), Harry Bath (Warrington), Lionel Cooper (Huddersfield), Ces Mountford (Wigan), Dave Valentine (Huddersfield), Duncan Jackson (Hull).

United Kingdom XIII versus French XIII, Parc Des Princes, 3 May 1951. Back: Charlie Winslade (Oldham), Don Robinson (Wakefield), Norman Hastings (Bradford), George Broughton (Castleford), Alan Prescott (St Helens), Jimmy Hayton (Workington), Ron Rylance (Dewsbury); front: Dave Valentine (Huddersfield), Joe Phillips (Bradford), Len Marson (Wakefield), Pat Devery (Huddersfield), Drew Turnbull (Leeds), Tommy Harrison (Salford), J. Milnes (masseur). (Courtesy *Rugby League Journal*)

1950–51 Championship table:

	P	W	D	L	Pts	F	A
France	3	2	0	1	4	53	30
Other Nationalities	3	2	0	1	4	65	47
England	3	2	0	1	4	46	48
Wales	3	0	0	3	0	38	77

Devery, now back to full fitness, captained a United Kingdom XIII to a 13–10 win against a French XIII on Thursday 3 May 1951 at Parc des Princes in Paris. In line with Other Nationalities, the team turned out in green jerseys, with and the selection included Australian, New Zealand, Welsh and Scottish players as well as Englishmen.

The significance of the game is not clear, but the date coincided with King George VI declaring the Festival of Britain open in a broadcast from the steps of St Paul's Cathedral in London. The line-up was: Joe Phillips (Bradford N), Drew Turnbull (Leeds), Pat Devery (Huddersfield), Norman Hastings (Bradford N), George Broughton (Castleford), Ron Rylance (Dewsbury), Tommy Harrison (Salford), Jimmy Hayton (Workington T), Len Marson (Wakefield T), Alan Prescott (St Helens), Don Robinson (Wakefield T), Charlie Winslade (Oldham), Dave Valentine (Huddersfield).

A couple of weeks later, two more games took place on Saturday 19 May as part of the Festival of Britain celebrations. Great Britain took on Australasia at Headingley, Leeds, and lost 23–20. The Great Britain side included Huddersfield pair Russ Pepperell and Dave Valentine, while Devery, Cooper and Henderson were in the Australasia team.

Great Britain: J. Evans (Hunslet), J. Hilton (Wigan), E. Ward (Bradford N), J. Broome (Wigan), T. Cook Halifax), E. Hesketh (St Helens), G.R. Pepperell (Huddersfield), K. Gee (Wigan), F. Osmond (Swinton), J. Booth (Wakefield T), N. Silcock (Wigan), G. Parsons (St Helens), D.D. Valentine (Huddersfield).
Scorers: Tries: Hilton, Pepperell, Booth, Parsons. Goals: E, Ward 4.
Australasia: J. Phillips (Bradford N), B. Bevan (Warrington), T. Allan (Leigh), P.C. Devery (Huddersfield), L.W. Cooper (Huddersfield), P. Henderson (Huddersfield), I. Proctor (Leeds), J. Payne (Hull), K. Kearney (Leeds), J.R. Mudge (Workington T), A.C. Clues (Leeds), O. Bevan (Warrington), M. Garbler (St Helens).
Scorers: Tries: Henderson 2, Bevan, Cooper, Garbler. Goals: Phillips 4.
Referee: Charlie Appleton (Warrington)
Attendance: 15,000

At the same time a Welsh XIII met an Empire XIII at Steboneath Park, Llanelli. The Empire team won 29–16 and included Hunter at full-back; Billy Banks turned out at scrum-half for Wales.

Welsh XIII: G.A. Moses (St Helens), A.H. Daniels (Halifax), G. Price (Halifax), L. Williams (Hunslet), R. Lambert (Dewsbury), J. Thomas (Workington T), W.M. Banks (Huddersfield), E. Gwyther (Belle Vue Rangers), R. Blakemore (St Helens), W.J. Jones (Llanelli), R. Cale (St Helens), B.V. Goldswain (Oldham), G. James (Hunslet).Substitute: D. John (Bridgend) for Moses
Scorers: Tries: Moses, Daniels, Price, Cale. Goals: Jones 2.
Empire XIII: J.C.H. Hunter (Huddersfield), W. Kindon (Leigh), J. Etty (Batley), G. Roughley (Wigan),J. McLean (Bradford N), W. Mather (Halifax), A. Burnell (Hunslet), A.G. Prescott (St Helens), H. Bradshaw (Dewsbury), J. Grainger (Salford), C. Thompson (Hunslet), M. Scott (Hull), R. Hughes (Wakefield T).
Scorers: Tries: Scott 2, Etty, Roughley, McLean, Grainger, Hughes.
Goals: Hunter 4.
Referee: D.L. Jones (Skewen)
Attendance: 6,500

The 1951–52 International Championship series included one of the most infamous matches in the history of the competition when France met Other Nationalities at Hull in front of an 18,000 crowd on Saturday 3 November 1951. It was a fierce encounter remembered as 'The Battle of The Boulevard'.

Lionel Cooper captained Other Nationalities to a glorious 17–14 win described as "a veritable bloodbath". Legendary Australian forward Arthur Clues was taken to hospital following a clash with his opposite number, Marseille policeman Eduoard Poncinet who knocked him out to settle an old score while the ball was still in the air from the kick-off. Clues was in a bad way, concussed with an injury to his eye.

Next, Peter Henderson of Huddersfield spent 20 minutes in the dressing room nursing a head injury before returning, second-row forward Burke of Leigh sustained a broken nose inflicted by Poncinet, which led to his dismissal by referee George Phillips 10 minutes from the end of the game.

The French side were in their prime, and played some brilliant rugby, but Other Nationalities had a pronounced forward superiority, with loose- forward Dave Valentine untiring.

Cooper, who inspired his side, played one of the greatest games of his career, scored three tries – the last of them a 'tightrope walk' down the touchline, and brushed aside three defenders on his way – while Devery kicked four goals. Together, they scored all the points for Other Nationalities. Puig-Aubert replied with four goals for France, and there was a try apiece from Cantoni and Bartoletti.

114

Other Nationalities 17 France 14 at The Boulevard, Saturday 3 November 1951. Lionel Cooper, receiving treatment to a knee injury from Hull masseur Jack Murray and a St John's Ambulance sergeant, with Bill Fallowfield (RFL secretary) next to him, John Daly, reserve forward for the Other Nationalities team, on the right.

On Saturday 1 December, Other Nationalities met Wales in Abertillery and won 22–11; the Huddersfield club was to the fore once again. Hunter, Devery, Cooper, Henderson and Valentine were included in the Other Nationalities side, while Billy Banks was the Welsh scrum-half. Pat Devery scored two tries and kicked a goal, and Cooper scored a try.

Eleven Australians were selected in the Other Nationalities side against England at Central Park, Wigan – which equalled their highest representation in 1949. The match was played on St George's Day, 23 April 1952, so it was perhaps appropriate that England emerged victorious 31–18.

A couple of weeks earlier, France had beaten Wales 20-12, so this was a title decider. If Other Nationalities won, they would claim the crown, if England won, the two teams and France would all be on four points, and yet again points difference would decide the title.

A great performance from Barrow stand-off Willie Horne won the game for England. Again, Huddersfield were well represented in both teams – Hunter, Cooper and Valentine for Other Nationalities, Dick Cracknell on the right wing for England.

1951–52 Championship table:

	P	W	D	L	Pts	F	A
France	3	2	0	1	4	76	42
England	3	2	0	1	4	79	71
Other Nationalities	3	2	0	1	4	57	56
Wales	3	0	0	3	0	34	77

During the early years of the code, many Northern Union representative and exhibition matches were played on association football clubs' grounds in various parts of the country in the hope of spreading interest in the new code – these efforts usually were not successful.

In later years the RFL turned to association football grounds again when interest in the Championship Finals reached the level that no rugby league ground – except Odsal – could accommodate the anticipated large post-war attendances. The Championship Finals were usually played at Maine Road, then the ground of Manchester City FC.

A further attempt to spread the sport was tried in London when the 1951–52 touring New Zealanders played a game against a British Empire XIII at Stamford Bridge, Chelsea, on Wednesday 23 January 1952 – the Empire side, which included Cooper and Valentine, emerged 26–2 winners before a crowd of 6,800.

A press comment about Lionel Cooper said: "McKinney and Ward combined to give the big Australian his first sight of the line, and a look usually means a try to Cooper. He thundered past White to score at the corner. Next time there were three men to beat, but Cooper got there again when any other man would have been pushed into touch... The Kiwi rally was killed by Cooper who snapped up a dropped pass on his own '25', beat White and held off all pursuit in a run of 75 yards'.

The teams were:

British Empire XIII: J. Cunliffe (Wigan), B. Bevan (Warrington), T. Allan (Leigh), E. Ward (Bradford N), L.W. Cooper (Huddersfield), J. Broome (Wigan), A.J. Pepperell (Workington T), F. Barton (Wigan), T. McKinney (Salford), A.G. Prescott (St Helens), A.H. Bath (Warrington) A.E. Clues (Leeds), D.D. Valentine (Huddersfield).

Scorers: Tries: Cooper 3, Bevan, Allan, Valentine. Goals: Ward 4.

New Zealand: D. White, J.R. Edwards, W.B.K. Hough, C.A. Eastlake, W. Sorenson, D.A. Barchard, J.S. Haig, C.R. Johnson, W.J. Davidson, D.L. Blanchard, C. McBride, D. Richards-Jolley, A.J. Atkinson.

Scorer: Goal: White.

Referee: Charlie Appleton (Warrington)

Other Nationalities in the meantime, had their revenge over England from the previous April when they defeated them 31–12 in the opening game of the 1952–53 European competition, played at Fartown on Saturday 18 October in front of 20,459.

It was almost a home game for the Other Nationalities team which included Hunter, Devery, Cooper, Henderson and Valentine, with Cooper as captain. Incidentally, one of the touch judges was Jack Liversidge, who was also from Huddersfield.

England were the first to attack with the help of a penalty, but though they got the ball they passed straight to Devery who in turn fed Henderson to race away – Ryder managed to tackle him as he looked likely to score, but from the play-the-ball Paskins sent Bevan over in the corner after only three minutes play, Devery's kick bounced on the cross-bar and over.

Ward and Dean tried hard to find openings without success, however, Other Nationalities were penalised and Ledgard kicked a goal from 40 yards out. England kept the pressure on when Other Nationalities dropped the ball and Castle kicked on. Cooper saved the situation before good work by Bath, Valentine and Cooper left the wingman with an open line, only to be recalled for a forward pass.

Minutes later Ledgard gathered the ball in his own half of the field and broke through; he kicked towards the right wing where Lewthwaite was ready; the ball bouncing well for him to gather and go over for a try. Ledgard converted. The England forwards looked the more dangerous, Blan broke away to give a reverse pass inside for Pawsey to score, again Ledgard kicked the goal to put England seven points ahead.

Within a minute Devery reduced the lead with a penalty and England, who got possession, kept up the attack until Devery found touch with a great rolling kick.

Virtually on half-time Bevan showed his class when he was hemmed in on the touchline 10 yards out. He sidestepped his way out of trouble to veer inside and scored by the posts. Devery kicked the goal to level the scores at 12–12. Fifteen minutes into the second period, Bevan scored his third try after he recovered a ball fumbled by England.

Then came a crucial turning point in the match. With the game about to enter the last quarter, Castle gathered a Henderson kick and broke clear, Lewthwaite carried on the move, but after cutting inside, was laid out and subsequently had to leave the field.

Injuries were starting to take their toll on England – with full-back

Ledgard struggling, Other Nationalities capitalised on the situation when Henderson came up on the outside of Cooper to score in the corner. Devery failed with the kick while scrum-half Toohey also came off for attention.

Though two men short, England found energy to attack, but Ledgard left the field with a damaged ankle just as Toohey returned, good play by Bath and Clues sent Bevan over for his fourth try – the most recorded by an Other Nationalities player – Bath kicked the goal. Shortly after, Henderson broke clear from half-way to score, again Bath kicked the goal to complete the rout.

Five weeks later, Other Nationalities travelled to the Stade Velodrome, Marseilles, on 23 November to take on France – this time Poncinet was missing from their line-up. Huddersfield were again well represented by Johnny Hunter, Pat Devery, Lionel Cooper, Peter Henderson and Dave Valentine.

A crowd of 17,611 saw centre Jacques Merquey score two tries and a couple of goals from Puig Aubert gave France a 10–6 half-time lead. In a contrasting second period France were completely outplayed as Other Nationalities rattled up 23 points without reply to give them an emphatic 29–10 win. Their tries came from Warrington's Brian Bevan with two, and one each from Devery, Cooper, Henderson, Valentine and Kelly. Harry Bath kicked four goals.

With two successes and one match remaining against Wales at Wilderspool, Warrington, on 15 April 1953, it seemed Other Nationalities were on target to claim their first European Championship. With Cooper captaining the side, Other Nationalities claimed their first International Championship in April 1953, albeit after a loss to Wales at Warrington. A superior points difference gave them the edge over Wales and England who also won two out of the three games played.

Joe Phillips took Hunter's place at full-back, and Ces Mountford replaced Henderson at stand-off. Devery and Cooper formed the left wing pairing with Valentine at loose-forward. Billy Banks was the Welsh scrum- half, so Huddersfield were well represented once again.

Other Nationalities, who had beaten Wales in all three previous encounters, led 13–7 at half-time. Cooper's try shortly after the resumption made it 16–7 and it all looked rosy, but Wales had other ideas and in an inspired finish tries from Williams, Tommy Harris and Norman Harris gave them victory 18–16.

Although they lost that game, Other Nationalities finished top of the

Championship Table on points scored difference – Wales and England also won two out of three – Cooper, as captain, received the Jean Galia Cup after the match.

1952–53 Championship table:

	P	W	D	L	Pts	F	A
Other Nationalities	3	2	0	1	4	76	40
Wales	3	2	0	1	4	48	51
England	3	2	0	1	4	46	52
France	3	0	0	3	0	39	66

In defence of their title, Other Nationalities' first game of the 1953–54 series was against Wales on Wednesday 7 October at Odsal. The attendance of 14,646 was the largest for a game between these two teams. Since the introduction of the Other Nationalities team into the International Championship in 1949–50, Wales and Other Nationalities had met four times to date.

Wales won only one of these games and that was at Wilderspool, Warrington, the previous April – the season in which Other Nationalities won the Jean Galia Trophy for the first time.

The trend didn't change as Other Nationalities, including Devery, Cooper and Valentine, easily accounted for Wales, who had Billy Banks at scrum-half, 30–5.

Extra interest was created by the fact that it was the first International Championship match to be played under floodlights. The game was also shown on BBC television. Other Nationalities had to forsake their traditional green jerseys for an all-white kit to make it easier for television viewers to distinguish between the two sides with the black and white pictures that were shown then.

Although close at the break – 9–5 to the Other Nationalities – Wales folded dramatically in the second half. Cooper helped himself to three tries, while Devery scored a try and added two goals – the 25 points margin equalled the 35–10 win against England at Central Park, Wigan, in April 1951.

Eleven days later Other Nationalities took on France at Stade Municipale, Bordeaux, and with Cooper and Valentine in the side triumphed 15–10.Although 10–5 down at half-time, Other Nationalities fought back with second half tries from Bevan and Robinson – 'fought' being the operative word as Clues and Poncinet faced each other again, although this time both stayed on the field.

Other Nationalities' final, and deciding, match of the 1953–54

International Championship was against England at Central Park, Wigan, on Saturday 28 November 1953 – both teams had won their opening two games.

The two teams had met in four previous encounters in which England came off second best. They had won only one of the four games, and scored 60 points against 97.

Two of these games were played at Central Park – in April 1951, when Other Nationalities swamped the hitherto unbeaten England team by 35–10 which handed the championship to France 'on a plate', and 12 months later when England gained revenge with a 31–18 win, once again the benefactor was France who were champions for the second successive year.

Again, Huddersfield were well represented in the Other Nationalities side by Devery, Cooper and Valentine, but the day belonged to England winger Peter Norburn – the Swinton player scored four tries.

England held a commanding lead 21–7 lead at half-time, but Other Nationalities rallied in the second half, however, not enough to prevent England winning by 30–22 and taking the title.

Other Nationalities 22 England 30 at Central Park 28 November 1953. Back: Wally Ellean (Rochdale Hornets), Brian Bevan (Warrington), Bevan Wilson (Workington), Arthur Clues (Leeds), Rex Mossop (Leigh), Dave Valentine (Huddersfield, Scot), John Mudge (Workington); front: Bob Dawson (Workington), Joe Phillips (Bradford, NZ), Lionel Cooper (Huddersfield), John Robinson (York, NZ), Tony Paskins (Workington), Pat Devery (Huddersfield). All Australians unless otherwise stated. (Courtesy David Middleton – League Information Services Ltd and Gary Lester)

1953–54 Championship table:

	P	W	D	L	Pts	F	A
England	3	3	0	0	6	61	32
Other Nationalities	3	2	0	1	4	67	45
France	3	1	0	2	2	38	44
Wales	3	0	0	3	0	32	77

On 3 January 1954, a Combined Nations team played France in Lyons to celebrate the 20th anniversary of French Rugby League. The Combined side included three American players and an Italian. Lionel Cooper was one of two Australians in the side, which lost 19-15. Seven countries were represented in the team, but curiously not New Zealand.

Due to the overseas signing ban being reimposed in 1947, Other Nationalities were finding themselves running short of numbers in 1954–55 – the majority of the side were approaching the veteran stage. In addition, the Welsh side participating in the four-team International Championship ceased to function in the International Championship of 1954–55 due to the reduction of Welsh players coming into the game, thus lacking strength in depth, this, plus the staging of the inaugural World Cup in France during the Autumn of 1954, resulted in the International Championship being suspended for the 1954–55 season.

The scrapping of the Wales and Other Nationalities sides had been subject to discussion in the past – in October 1952, having opposed each other for the first time the previous May in Paris, discussions between the Rugby Football League and their French counterparts had muted a three-Test series between the countries – the plan being to replace the existing four-team International Championship, however, at the time this never materialised.

A representative game played after the World Cup was between a Rugby League XIII and Australasia at Odsal Stadium, Bradford, on Wednesday 17 November 1954. Cooper and Valentine played for the home side, but Australasia won 25–13. Cooper scored a try.
Northern Rugby League XIII: J. Phillips (Bradford N), B. Bevan (Warrington), A. Paskins (Workington T), T.W. Lynch (Halifax), L.W. Cooper (Huddersfield), P. Metcalfe (St Helens), G.J. Helme (Warrington), A.G. Prescott (St Helens), A. Wood (Leeds), D. Robinson (Wakefield T), A.C. Clues (Hunslet), A.H. Bath (Warrington), D.D. Valentine (Huddersfield).

Scorers: Tries: Bevan 2, Cooper. Goals: Bath 2.

Australasia: C.B. Churchill (Australia), C.A. Eastlake (New Zealand), A. Watson (Australia), R.J. McKay (New Zealand), I. Moir (Australia), R. Banks (Australia), K. Holman (Australia), R. Bull (Australia), K. Kearney (Australia), W.R. McLennan (New Zealand), P. Diversi (Australia), K. O'Shea (Australia), A.J. Atkinson (New Zealand)

Scorers: Tries: Watson 2, Banks, Kearney, O'Shea. Goals: McKay 5.

Referee: C.F. Appleton (Warrington)

Attendance: 17,049 (£2,505)

After the break in 1954–55, a decision was made to allow Welshmen to be selected in the Other Nationalities team for the forthcoming 1955–56 International Championship tournament – which was only destined for one more season – ironically, Other Nationalities clinched the Championship for the second time. Devery and Cooper had retired, and Hunter was not selected for Other Nationalities. Billy Banks and Dave Valentine both played, while Mick Sullivan and Brian Briggs played for England in the series.

11. Testimonials: Lionel Cooper

Excerpts from Lionel Cooper's testimonial booklet, published by the Huddersfield C & A.C. Supporters Club, compiled by A.N. Gaulton in 1955.

Foreword

I welcome this opportunity to give Lionel Cooper my best wishes for the success of his Testimonial Fund. I have seen so many great wings in my playing clays, but to Lionel Cooper I must give pride of place. He is the strongest winger I have ever seen, and lie will be a great loss to our club when he retires from the game. Strong on the attack, running with the greatest determination, and seeming to find that bit of extra speed when needed, he also has a peach of a side-step. The great number of tries he has scored for Huddersfield shows how much Lionel has done to keep the name of our club one of the best in the League. He has everything that makes a great player of the game, a good team man and always willing to play the game.

I am sure the Football Committee are with me in wishing Lionel a great success with the Testimonial Fund.

Ben Gronow (Chairman, Football Committee)

Personal Tributes to Lionel Cooper

Rich as the colours of a great club

Rich wine and rich metal are represented in the colours of the great club that has its home at Fartown, and equally rich in merit have been the many great players who have come from the Dominions of the Commonwealth of Empire to help achieve many successes on the playing fields of England.

First among wingers, we had Rosenfeld, and later Mills and Markham – all great wingers who were prolific scorers. And now, with the post-war years, has come Lionel Cooper another great winger who shone as brightly as any of the Australians who preceded him. Great player, great sportsman, and great citizen. Could any better words he used in description of the merits of a man who will never be forgotten at Fartown – especially as a good citizen and sportsman. May his testimonial reward him as he deserves.

I first heard of Lionel when I flew out to Australia in 1946 for the *Sunday Dispatch* and the Sydney *Sun* to cover the tour of the British Lions led by Gus Risman. Cooper had come to the front very suddenly in the post war revival of football, and his success in that season in all the big games resulted in him being named as the player-of-the-year. No wonder several English clubs sought his signature to a contract ... Leeds were in the race, but he decided to come to Fartown where he has won almost every honour possible, even to the captaincy of the Other Nationalities team when they finished up victorious against England, France and Wales for the Jean Galia Memorial Cup.

Lionel had the distinction of playing for his state of New South Wales in 1945 after only six games of grade football.

Let me quote what Ernie Christensen wrote of him in his R.L. Annual after Cooper was named as "The Player of the Year" in Sydney in 1946.

"Australia's outstanding player last season in matches of all types was Lionel Cooper, left winger in all three test matches and in every match played by New South Wales

"Cooper had the honour, with Joe Jorgensen, of being the only players in the State chosen for every representative match played. To add to this performance he scored in all these matches with the exception of the third test. His tries against England in the first test and against Queensland in Brisbane came from 80 yards runs and were regarded as amongst the best of the season.

"Cooper has been popular with League followers in both New South Wales and Queensland because he has all the attributes of a class athlete. He plays hard, yet always 300 per cent clean, never questions decisions and is always ready to learn from his coaches. His team spirit is such that he will play in any position he is asked and at any time."

That was an Australian opinion before Lionel came to Fartown to serve the "Claret and Gold" in the excellent manner he has done for so many seasons. We can all endorse it.

Harry Sunderland
(The *Sunday Dispatch* and BBC commentator)

An outstanding captain

To pay tribute to as great a player and sportsman as Lionel Cooper in just a few lines is a near impossibility. A strong runner with a great burst of speed, he has proved himself a potential match-winner in many matches for Huddersfield during the past eight years.

I have had the pleasure of playing with Lionel and against him, but I think the most enjoyable matches were playing together for Other Nationalities. He is an outstanding captain, and always does his best on the field of play. A notable feature is his burst in from touch to make play for the right-wing, surely the essence of a great and unselfish player.

It was a big loss to Australia when Lionel left his native country, but a great gain for the Huddersfield club and English rugby league football when he arrived in England. May the future of this prolific scoring winger prove long and continue successful.

My sincere best wishes, Lionel, for a record-breaking testimonial.
Brian Bevan, Warrington

Through the rugby league text book
In the space of eight years Lionel Cooper has scored well over 400 tries for Huddersfield Rugby League Club. An outstanding memory for his countless admirers must be Nos. 400 to 404, which were chalked-up against Wakefield Trinity earlier this season. As though to celebrate the passing of a milestone he squeezed the achievements of those eight years into a 45-minute potted demonstration of the qualities which place him securely among the best two or three wingers who have ever played the game.

It was opportunist Cooper who scored No. 400. Hirst the Trinity full-back, was better placed than he to reach the ball when Sullivan kicked it over the line, but it was the energetic Cooper who got his hands on it when they dived simultaneously.

No. 401, four minutes later, went to sidestepper Cooper. He had Hirst to beat again after taking Griffin's pass. Hirst set himself for a hefty bump but found himself grasping shadows as Cooper's massive frame was flicked skilfully inside him off the left foot. (Incidentally, when Cooper gives the impression of running "through" a tackle it is as often as not this miniature, perfectly controlled side-step which beats the defender. Spectators are apt to miss it).

Two minutes after everyman Cooper had been given an easy run to the line for No. 402 ("I could have scored it myself," said the man behind me). Bulldozer Cooper put on the party piece. He was challenged four times in a 40-yard run, but he kept going in a straight line for No. 403. The challengers might as well have tried to pull the Royal Scot off the rails.

No. 404 was a repetition of No. 400 on a rather grander scale, and Trinity were left wondering how they would have fared but for this superman. Well enough to have won, perhaps.

Alfred Drewry of the *Yorkshire Post*

Magnificent temperament

I have had many privileges in my rugby career, most of them at Fartown. But the outstanding one has been that of associating and playing alongside one of rugby league's most forceful and brilliant stars – Lionel Cooper.

Since this burly Australian joined the H.C. & A.C. along with Johnny Hunter, he has stormed his way into the annals of Fartown and the Rugby League in the most devastating style I have ever witnessed on a rugger field. His determined attitude in the face of over whelming opposition, the speed and skill in which he disposed of the keenest defensive cover and his ability to pull out the match winning effort when urgently required, has always been a delight and source of admiration to me as captain and coach of the team for some years.

Lionel will live in my memory long after his playing days are over and his prolific scoring feats are already firmly inscribed in the records of Fartown.

I feel particularly indebted to Lionel as he has been a major influence in many honours that came my way. I recall that great day at Wembley, 1953, when we were being sorely pressed and Pat Devery was injured and resting on the wing. I called upon Lionel to take a kick at goal which would give us the lead at that critical time. The responsibility was tremendous but his calm acceptance and ease with which he kicked that goal was a great tribute to his magnificent temperament.

Thank you Lionel for the brilliant displays you have given us, for your leadership and inspiration, and I sincerely hope your testimonial is worthy of your great name and reputation.

Russ Pepperell, Huddersfield

Intelligent change of pace

Sidney H. Crowther ("Autolycus" of the *Huddersfield Examiner*)

It is easy to imagine that nothing today is quite as good as it used to be, and to drop into the way of thinking "they were greater in the old days." The general standards of play today may not be as good as they were, but those who are watching the rugby league game will be able to tell their boys as they grow up that the years that followed the Second World War were rich in great wingers.

"Cooper and Bevan" they will exclaim. "Why, lad, they don't breed men like that nowadays!"

It is not easy to understand why the greatest of the wing players have come from Australia – Rosenfeld, Horder, Harris, Mills, Markham, Bevan and Cooper. Oh, yes, there have been some fine English and Welsh wingers, but none of them quite in the same class as the great Australians, except, perhaps, for Ellaby.

Lionel Cooper came into the game comparatively late in life for a footballer, and though he had gained test match honours in Australia, when the Huddersfield club persuaded him to travel to England, he was not then as great a player as he later became. After all he had been playing the game for rather less than two years.

He did not impress in his first game as did Hunter, who settled down immediately, and some Fartown followers were a little disappointed with him.

Cooper was in those days a straight runner with a powerful hand-off, and he ran himself in gradually. He came here with a reputation but he was very willing to learn new tricks, and since those days he has found a swerve, and developed a side-step.

It was at a match at the Boulevard that he first found his swerve. I remember the occasion because I wrote in the report for the Saturday evening *Examiner*, that he swerved round Fred Miller, and on my return to Huddersfield was taken to task by Fartowners who said in effect, "Go on with you, Cooper can't swerve!"

He did then and he has done since. That particular one was a beauty, and the Hull spectators were cross. They said that Miller ought to have had him!

Although we are bound to class Cooper among the great wing men to be seen within a life-time, he has not all the gifts we expect of a man in that position—but then no-one has!

He is not, as wingmen go, very fast. He hasn't the power of taking evasive action such as that possessed by Brian Bevan, but in a dash for the corner he can beat as many men as Bevan.

He does it differently, of course. He has a stronger physique that makes him more difficult to hold, but though some of his tries may seem to be the result of sheer power, it would be entirely wrong to put down his qualities as a wing merely to personal strength.

He has a powerful and often precisely timed hand-off, he has at times an amazing way of disposing of a tackler, and he has also a shake of his thigh from which the opponent who has gone for him bounces off like a man thrown from a horse.

None of us, I imagine, have ever seen anything like the last attribute in football before.

Besides all these gifts he also beats opponents by intelligent change of pace. How often have we seen him start a try-scoring run at a trot, drawing the opposition before he tried to beat it? He can outwit an opponent by the movement of his feet as well.

Of some wings who score many tries we can say, "He ought to with such a centre! " But without in any way trying to belittle the centres who have played alongside him, the remarkable feature of Cooper's tally of tries is that so many of them have been entirely his own.

He hasn't been a mere finisher; he's made an opening where none seemed to exist, and got through against all odds and expectations.

The memory of some of his tries will remain with many a rugby league enthusiast – and not merely Fartowners – for years to come, and the response to the Cooper Testimonial should be worthy of the innumerable thrills he has given to the rugby league public.

Devastating hand-off

The Huddersfield club have long been renowned in rugby league circles for providing their own supporters and, indirectly, followers of the game in general, with some of the brightest stars which the rugby code has produced in this country or abroad. They could hardly have foreseen, however, the tremendous impact Lionel Cooper would make on our game, for he has been outstanding among even the great wealth of talent from the Dominions.

When the talk turns to rugby league wingmen one immediately thinks of Brian Bevan, a countryman of Lionel's, but just as Brian shines with the adroit side step and pulsating burst of speed so Lionel excels with the devastating hand-off and the powerful run. In different ways both are brilliant, both spectacular, and certainly rank as two of the finest wingers in the history of the game.

To recall one's outstanding memory of Lionel is indeed a difficult task. He has thrilled us so many times, scored so many remarkable tries and done so many wonderful things in our rugby league games since he came here from Australia in 1947.

But I shall never forget two of his triumphs. The first was at The Boulevard, Hull, on November 3rd, 1951. On that day Lionel was captain of Other Nationalities and they defeated France for the first time. The score was 17-14 – and what a battle it was!

Arthur Clues was taken to hospital after three minutes following a clash with Poncinet, later to be sent off; Peter Henderson was off for 20 minutes of the second half with a head wound which required five stitches; Jeff Burke had his nose broken; Dave Valentine got a kick in his back; Tony Paskins and Lionel himself were limping; and Bob McMaster's face was covered in blood.

The French pulled no punches and naturally some of "The Others" were wanting to "mix it" but captain Cooper's wise counsel: "Keep on playing football," prevailed, and so did Other Nationalities.

A headline I read: "Cooper's great leadership of 12 heroes" summed it all up. Lionel scored Other Nationalities' three tries that day, the last of them after a "tightrope walk" along the touchline, during which he brushed aside three defenders, and Pat Devery kicked four goals just to make it a real Fartown "do." At the end of the match Lionel was warmly congratulated by all his team-mates for a wonderful display.

The other triumph is more recent – and in it Lionel did not score a try, which is news in itself. It was at Wembley on April 25th, 1953, when Huddersfield won the Rugby League Challenge Cup with their 15–10 defeat of St Helens. Johnny Hunter had just been carried off and Pat Devery was limping and unable to kick goals, but Billy Banks had just made the scores 8–8 with a grand solo try and it was vital that Huddersfield should obtain the goal – and the lead.

They did, thanks to Lionel, who calmly thumped the ball straight between the posts from a non-too-easy angle. That goal, I believe, was a tonic to the Huddersfield players and from then on they never looked like losing even though St Helens got two more points.

Lionel got another goal before the end – just to prove the first was not a fluke – a remarkable achievement by a player who had not been kicking regularly and whose only two previous goals of the season were in the third game of the term.

The toast is Lionel Cooper who has so enriched the history of British rugby league. Good health, good luck and best wishes to him.
Jack Bentley of the *Daily Dispatch*

What a winger!
"So they are giving Lionel Cooper a testimonial. It may seem trite to say one is hardly surprised, for here is a player who has given great pleasure to countless thousands. I first heard the name of Lionel

Cooper mentioned when his name was linked with that of the Leeds club. Leeds were certainly hot on his track, and I remember the late Mr George Ibbetson, secretary at Headingley, telling me that Cooper was 'more or less fixed up'. But they didn't land their fish – instead he was snapped up by Huddersfield, and as year after year he has run in his high quota of tries, many of them of the kind one remembers for a long time, so he has made the Leeds officials more and more regret the hesitancy that caused them to miss him.

With such a player we may all have different opinions, but the games distinguished by Cooper's exploits that will stand out forever in my mind were Hunslet v Huddersfield, at Parkside on 6 October 1950, and Other Nationalities v France, at Hull on 3 November 1951.

The first of these was a cup-tie, the semi-final of the Yorkshire Cup, which Huddersfield won by 20–7. In the first half Cooper got the ball and there were at least five opponents in front of him. He beat two by side-step and swerve, handed off a third, went through the fourth and then, with quite the most spectacular and longest dive I've ever seen, sails past the last bewildered defender like the man on the flying trapeze. So there, in one effort, you had everything it is possible to see in an attacking winger. Throughout that game, in which he scored two tries, Cooper demanded the attention of two or three players each time he got the ball.

Just over a year later I was sitting in the stand at The Boulevard. Very early on Arthur Clues of Leeds had been carried off in what we came to call 'the Poncinet incident'.

Brian Bevan was having a rough time of it on the right flank as the Frenchmen tore about the field, and things hardly looked bright for Other Nationalities since Cooper, on the left wing, had a thigh injury.

It became a grim fight indeed, but although short-handed, Other Nationalities won through to as great a victory as one could wish to see. How so? Cooper did it.

Scorning his injury he leapt to the attack three times.

On each occasion a trail of would-be tacklers were left behind, and the brilliant flanker from New South Wales scored all three tries which, with four goals from Pat Devery, enabled them to gain a 17–14 success.

These are the two matches I vividly recall, but big Li has given many, many more thrills than those I have recounted – and I've never yet met a rugby league fan who has not said of him 'what a winger!"

Arthur Haddock of the *Yorkshire Evening News*

Power and thrust

It gives me great pleasure to be able to pay tribute to a great footballer. I'm sure there will never be another player like him. No doubt we shall see some great wingers don the claret and gold in the future, but will there be one with the power and thrust of my long-time friend and team-mate, Lionel?

He has scored his tries in every conceivable way. His trump card has been his terrific power and neat side-step, but he has also run from his own "25" to touch down.

Lionel has been always first to help in other players' testimonials. He has driven his car literally thousands of miles to help at various dances, benefits, etc., and deserves every success in his own benefit. We, his team-mates, shall miss him when he retires, as no doubt the Fartown supporters will. I salute a great player and a good friend. Good luck, Lionel!

Dave Valentine, Huddersfield

Delivers the goods

During the first post war tour of Australia in 1946 I saw a number of Australian players whom I realised would do well in English football. On my return home I was asked my opinion of certain players. The Leeds club were after Lionel Cooper, a strong winger who had scored tries against the British team in both the first and second tests.

The Huddersfield club asked me if I could help them to get a winger to follow in the wake of other famous Australian wingers like Rosenfeld, Mills, Markham, etc., who had graced the Claret and Gold Jersey with distinction. I pin-pointed Cooper and the Huddersfield committee asked me if I would do the deal for them. I contacted Ray Stehr, the former Australian test forward who had 'found' Cooper playing in Army Rugby League. One of the conditions in signing Cooper was the attachment of a full-back called Johnny Hunter. Of course Huddersfield were in the dark about both Cooper and Hunter but they believed in my judgement and authorised the signing of this pair at a price well under the £2,000 mark What a bargain!

Lionel Cooper's success at Huddersfield is clearly indicated in his try-scoring records. Like his fellow Australian try-scoring machine, Brian Bevan of Warrington, many of Lionel's tries have had to be scored even when he got the ball.

Unlike Brian Bevan, Lionel Cooper looks the part with his fine physique but, like Bevan, proceeds to deliver the goods when in

131

possession. Many fine players have graced the famous Fartown jersey, Lionel Cooper takes his place amongst the best for excellent wing play and the provider of thrilling tries.

I feel I did Huddersfield a particularly good turn when both Cooper and Hunter were persuaded to join the Fartown club. It also makes me feel what a pity that a ban is in existence and the likelihood of future Coopers in English football is a little remote.

Eddie Waring

(*Sunday Pictorial* columnist and BBC television commentator)

My sporting life

Although I played most of the sports under the sun way back its Australia, I feel that my sporting life really began in earnest when I joined Huddersfield. Having been asked to pinpoint my more memorable moments, I must say that I will always remember the wonderful spectacle of treading on the Wembley turf for the first time and the tremendous thrill of having obtained a winner's medal. None the less will I remember having captained the Other Nationalities' side in the year they won the International Championship, having the honour of captaining the British Empire team when playing at Stamford Bridge, Chelsea, against the New Zealand side in 1952, and the occasion when, as captain of the Huddersfield side, we were successful in winning the Yorkshire Cup at Headingley.

My best game for the Huddersfield club? One in particular stands out in my mind – the semi-final of the Yorkshire Cup at Hunslet in 1950 when I was successful in scoring two tries. Then, of course, I can look with a tremendous amount of pleasure on the wonderful team spirit – which existed on the day that I scored 10 tries against Keighley to break the club record held by Ray Markham.

Speaking of records, and referring to more recent events, I am proud, very proud indeed, to have had the honour to be the one to break my fellow country-man, Albert Rosenfeld's record of scoring the record number of tries for the Huddersfield club. In the eight years that I have been with Huddersfield my efforts on the field and the tries that I have scored, whether they have been walk-ins or something a little more spectacular, could not have been achieved without the co-operation of the other 12 members of the side. It is a team game and as a team game the whole 13 men are responsible in every way for the achievements of the team.

Reverting to international matches and speaking of team spirit I would like to recall what was later termed the "Battle of the Boulevard," Other Nationalities v. France at Hull. What a game that was and what spirit!

Rugby league has opened up many avenues in life for me and in some instances has been responsible for the opportunities to meet leading sportsmen in athletics, cricket, golf, soccer, swimming and rugby league. What a great maker of friendships sport is.

In my own game I have played against many great players, and having been asked to name a post-war team in which I would have liked to play, I would select the following:

M. Ryan, B. Bevan, E. Ward, P. Devery, L. Cooper, W. H. T. Davies, G. Helme, K. Gee, J. Egan, F. Whitcombe, A. Clues, T. Foster, D. Valentine.
Reserves: I. Owens, M. Sullivan.

I mention Mick Sullivan as a reserve because in my eight years in English football I feel he is the best prospect I have seen. Speed, brains, courage, determination and, above all, a willingness to learn, in fact all the essentials of a great player.

My sporting life has indeed been full and has provided me with opportunities I would never have dreamed of; a trip to England and visits to France, together with the chance to shape my life for years to come. My success can be attributed to so many factors and my thanks are due, firstly, to the officials and players of the Huddersfield club for the encouragement which they have given me over that period; to the members of the Fartown Supporters' Club, and to all Huddersfield "died-in-the wool" rugby league enthusiasts for the wonderful support which von have given me, and to the press for their encouragement.

Now Anno Domini and the middle age spread is unfortunately catching up with me, I know that my sporting life is gradually drawing to a close, and I would like to finish by saying on behalf of my wife and myself, "Thank you Huddersfield for having us, for making us welcome, and may I, in return, wish in the future years that Huddersfield will still be a household word wherever good, open rugby league football is played."

Lionel Cooper

Lionel Cooper was appointed coach at Dewsbury for the 1956–57 season.
The Dewsbury team pictured are: back: Cooper (trainer-coach), C. Waterson,
D. Cox, G. Popplewell, H. Grainger, D. Cawthra, J. Farrar, T. Danter;
front: J. Curley, J. Clark, P. Todd (c), E. Lea, R. Taylor, F. Millican.

12. Testimonials: Johnny Hunter

Excerpts from Johnny Hunter's testimonial booklet, published by the Huddersfield C & A.C. Supporters Club, compiled by A.N. Gaulton in 1955.

Foreword

I well remember, in February, 1947, calling in at the Fartown Pavilion and being introduced by my father to a new Fartown player by the name of Johnny Hunter. Little did I realise that in the very near future I, together with a big following of Fartown supporters, was to see the same man introduce to our game a new type of full back play which created such enthusiasm and surprise to all who had the pleasure of seeing Johnny when he was really in the peak period of his career.

His fielding and catching of a ball has, in my humble opinion, never been surpassed, and what brought the crowds to their toes more than when he commenced one of those telling runs through the opposition.

This season, up to the time of his unfortunate knee injury, Johnny has been helping us out on the wing and not letting his side down in any way. He is the right type of player to have in any dressing room as he is blessed with a pleasing personality and is most helpful to the junior members of the team. From his first appearance at Fartown Johnny has always been eager and willing to serve the club in any capacity.

It is indeed a pleasure to have the opportunity of contributing to this Souvenir Brochure and I would like to convey my own personal good wishes to Johnny and also, on behalf of the Football Committee, wish him all that he could wish for himself.

Hubert Lockwood (Chairman, Football Committee)

Personal Tributes to Johnny Hunter

Great capacity for doing the unexpected

It is not easy to find a single adjective to fit Johnny Hunter. He is very individual, like no one else who ever donned a claret and gold jersey, and though a fitting successor to a great line of full backs we have had at Fartown, there is in him no point of comparison with any one of them. He does things like picking up the ball with one hand that no-one else would dare, and he does it with as few mistakes or knocks—on as any full-back who takes his time and uses both hands.

He has a great capacity for doing the unexpected. Few players in recent times have so often made a crowd gasp because he has done the last thing anybody, either on the field of play or round the touch lines, expected. Even his errors, like his strokes of success, have fallen within the category of unaccountable.

There never was anything of dull science about Johnny. He takes risks—few full backs more so, but always for the sake of enterprise. Yet he is essentially as level-headed as any Australian who ever came to England. If he takes risks it is never because he is reckless, but because by temperament he knows that you'll never get much out of football unless you play it adventurously.

And, of course, he's right. Johnny has got a lot out of football. You get the impression many a time as he sets off on one of his runs that he's really enjoying a bit of fun. There is a lot of the schoolboy left in him that pops out when he plays rugby.

That's why he and Puig Aubert, the French full back, have been the two most entertaining footballers of these times. And I use the word entertaining in no disparaging sense. I mean simply that both of them have given us thrills of an unexpected kind, that they have had the rare gift of making a game interesting and full of character merely because they were taking part in it.

Johnny has had some training as a boxer and he knows how to use his fists, but you never see him raise a hand where he shouldn't. He's too level headed – and an exception among men who are level minded in that inspiration often comes to him.

He's popular on "away" grounds as well as at Fartown – so much so that it has been rare indeed for away" spectators ever to get angry with him. He's a sportsman in every sense of the word.

Sidney H. Crowther "Autolycus" of the _Huddersfield Examiner_

Exuberant and carefree style

Fartowners have been extremely fortunate in post war years in having secured from Australia and New Zealand players of such outstanding ability as Cooper, Devery, Hunter and Henderson. These brilliant players have helped to enhance the already distinguished records of Fartown.

We have appreciated them all in their own rights but none has given more pleasure to the spectator than Johnny Hunter. His exuberant and carefree style – his uncanny sense of timing which enables him to take the most difficult ball from the air or the ground, with apparent ease – and by his elusive running bringing his team from defence to attack, have been a source of wonder and admiration since he joined us in 1947. I had the pleasure of befriending Johnny when he first arrived in Huddersfield and the ensuing years have proved what must have been apparent to all who have seen him play – that he is a sportsman in the truest sense of the word and a gentleman at all times.

It therefore gave me great pleasure to hear that his loyal service is to be justly rewarded by a "Testimonial" and I trust that it proves to be a happy and successful event. I conclude by wishing Johnny and his family good health, prosperity and several more years at Fartown.

Russ Pepperell, Huddersfield, Cumberland and England

Cavalier spirit

I wrote in an Australian magazine called *Sport* some months ago an article on John Hunter. Amongst the things I said of him were, 'There have been better players than Hunter at Fartown from Australia, but none who have given more entertainment to the crowd and played rugby in the same cavalier spirit." And paying tribute now to Johnny, who is having a well-deserved testimonial, I can only endorse what I previously wrote.

I could tell many stories of this "lad" whom I was instrumental in bringing to Huddersfield along with Lionel Cooper. I had seen Hunter playing in an unimportant match on the Sydney Cricket ground and when Huddersfield decided to sign Cooper and another player was offered I was reminded by Ray Stehr about this game that Hunter had played. My memory was sufficiently strong enough to realise he would be an asset to the Fartown club and my judgement has been proved accurate.

I can still recall that cold, frosty day on the Huddersfield platform when we met the pair in after their trip from Australia. One female fan waiting said of Johnny, "Doesn't he look a happy lad?" And that is 'J.H.'

He plays football in a happy way and his contributions to English football have been of such a character we shall be sorry when the day arrives when he hangs his boots up for good. A first class sport, a first class footballer and a rugby gentleman—what more can I say.

Eddie Waring (*Sunday Pictorial*)

Brilliant unorthodoxy

When rugby fans talk about attacking full-backs Johnny Hunter's name is one which invariably crops up. "The best catcher of a ball I have ever seen," they say. His bursts up the middle from the full-back position have given the spectators at Fartown many a thrilling moment.

Johnny's brilliant unorthodoxy had much to do with Fartown's great post-war record in which Johnny has won every medal available to a player with a Yorkshire team. Along with the players at Fartown I wish Johnny every success in his testimonial.

Dave Valentine
Huddersfield, Other Nationalities and Great Britain

Hair-raising bursts

Perhaps the testimonial which Johnny Hunter will cherish most is that his successor at full-back in the Huddersfield team, Frank Dyson, thinks the world of him. It is not often that the ambitious understudy reveres the star who stands in his path to fame, but then, it is not often that the star tutors the understudy to the extent that Johnny has helped Frank. It is in no small measure due to the hours that these two have spent together in practice that the youngster is now a candidate for higher representative honours. Need I say more about Hunter the man?

Hunter the full-back came to Fartown with Lionel Cooper early in 1947, but whereas Cooper had already achieved test honours, Hunter was an unknown quantity. Even we who had been on the tour with Risman's team in 1946 knew little about him, for it was not until we were almost on the point of leaving Australia that he made the grade in the Eastern Suburbs senior team. Hunter had watched Martin Ryan demonstrate the then new technique of the full-back who never kicked. He did not copy Ryan slavishly, but he still did more running than kicking. And what running. Who will ever forget those hair-raising bursts to take the loose ball at full speed? His fearlessness cost him several bouts of concussion, but it also paved the way for many a spectacular Fartown try, and it is a tribute to his mettle that he went in just as fearlessly next time. As the years passed he learned discretion, but never at the cost of valour. And whoever has seen him commit an act in the slightest degree questionable? Huddersfield have been lucky in the players they have brought from Australia. They have never had a more loyal clubman than Johnny Hunter.

A.L. Drewry (*The Yorkshire Post*)

A tonic to the team

It is indeed a privilege for me to have the opportunity of writing a few lines on Johnny's behalf. Our rugby league careers commenced together in Australia, and during the past 10 years I have seen Johnny give many brilliant performances and possibly give more entertainment value on a rugby league football field than any player in post-war football.

In the early days Johnny was a centre but always had a liking for the full-back position and I feel that no-one will contradict me when I say that had it not been for an early season injury he would most certainly have been Australia's full back in the 1946 Test series against Great Britain. It was only fitting, therefore, that he should gain the honours that he has gained since coming to England, and they have been many.

There have, from time to time, been critics who have said that he was too venturesome and that as the last line of defence he should have adopted safety tactics, but suffice it to say, that having been one of his team mates it was a tonic to the team every time Johnny ventured into the threequarters or set off on one of his long weaving runs into the opposition's territory.

It is hard to compare contemporary players with old timer's but I think everyone will agree that Johnny's catching of a ball high in the air or the brilliant scooping up of a greasy ball from the feet of oncoming forwards has not had its equal in the rugby league game. These two aspects, combined to the tremendous fillip he gave to the team when he returned to the field at Wembley in 1953 in the memorable match against St Helens will long live in my memory.

Johnny had a reputation in Australia as a lovable character and a first class all round sportsman and that reputation has been enhanced still further in this country by his displays not only on the football field – where he has played in any position required of him – but also on the cricket field, and the manner in which he has conducted himself off the field.

There is no question about his popularity with the Huddersfield officials and his team mates, but to be popular with opponents and their spectators in any form of sport is a very difficult thing. I feel it is no exaggeration to say that Johnny can class this as one of his achievements.

In conclusion, I would like to say thank you, Johnny, for your sincerity in our friendship and may your testimonial be the success that

your efforts, your enthusiasm and your team spirit so richly deserves.
Lionel Cooper
Huddersfield, Other Nationalities and Australia

Quality of fearlessness

Most overseas players have come into the Northern R.L. game with a fanfare. Not so Johnny Hunter. He was quite the "lesser light" on arrival at Fartown with his famous countryman, Lionel Cooper.

I well remember dashing across from Leeds to Huddersfield with a photographer to take a picture of the two newcomers from Australia. "Who's the other chap," I asked, pointing to Johnny. "That's Hunter – he's a full back," came the reply.

And, at that time, few know little more than this about the man who was to develop into yet another brilliant Huddersfield star. It wasn't long before Hunter was answering all the questions in the best possible way – by sterling performances on the field.

Not only has Hunter been one of the best full-backs ever to wear the "claret and gold" but he very quickly showed that in addition to possessing abundant skill he was endowed with what sportsmen are pleased to call "a big heart".

Few players have displayed greater courage on the football field; as an attacker or defender Hunter has never been known to quit. That quality of fearlessness has in the course of his career brought him more than the normal quota of injuries, but he has always come back smiling.

In short, then, Johnny Hunter has been, and continues to be, a grand personality; a credit to Australia and to the famous club with which he came to prominence.
Arthur Haddock (*Yorkshire Evening News*)

Miraculous handling and catching

Way back in Australia, Johnny Hunter used to talk about coming to England to play rugby league football, but he was told: 'You won't do any good over there'. How wrong were those dismal prophets!

Even so it was mainly as a companion for Lionel Cooper that Johnny came here, for Fartown badly wanted Lionel, who did not fancy coming by himself. Thus Huddersfield told Johnny to come along too – 'But it was the other fellow they wanted', Johnny once told me.

Fartown's luck was in, however, and so was Johnny's in a way, for in his own brand of rugby league – at full back – he turned out to be just about as much of an attraction as that 'other fellow'.

He wasn't always a full-back and for some of the many thrills that he has given them, rugby league followers over here owe something to that great Australian cricketer, Ray Lindwall. Ray is a good friend of Johnny's and it was he who gave Johnny many tips about the art of full-back play, for Lindwall was a first-class No. 1.

But no matter how many tips Lindwall gave to the young Hunter they would not have been much use without the obvious flair for the full-back position which Johnny undoubtedly possessed.

Kicking is usually reckoned to be one of the necessary attributes of a full-back, and yet Johnny has excelled in the position without shining particularly as a kicker. The Hunter brand of full-back play is, indeed, peculiar to Johnny Hunter. It is hazardous and thrilling, spectacular and profitable, as all who have seen Johnny play will know, especially Fartown supporters who have often seen him return to the field bandaged or strapped up, to plunge once more into the fray.

He would indeed be a dull dog who has not been excited by Johnny's miraculous handling and catching of the ball as he tears at full speed cross-field, and it would be an unappreciative fan, whether he supports Huddersfield or their opponents, who has failed to be stirred by Johnny's remarkable clearing runs up the middle.

One can always expect the unexpected from Johnny Hunter and for that alone he deserves the thanks of rugby league followers in this country, for it is football genii like him who keep the turnstiles clicking.

His tries, as a full back, at least have generally had some remarkable quality about them and I well remember one at Hunslet in the 1951–52 season. Incidentally, that 'other fellow' also reckons this is a super try and he knows something about try-scoring, but I'll tell you about it in Johnny's own words.

They are an eloquent example of his kind of football – snappy, and to the point. 'I got possession from a play-the-ball on our own line and managed to score at the other end'.

That's all there was to it as far as Johnny was concerned! The very best of luck to him.

Jack Bentley (*The Daily Dispatch*)

The right approach

It is good to hear that the Huddersfield Club is giving Johnny Hunter a testimonial. I have played with and against Johnny on many occasions and it will be generally agreed that he brings the right approach to any game in which he takes part. His approach has been one of adventure, tinged perhaps with recklessness at times, but none will decry him for that. Rugby league football is a man's game. We all take risks and let ourselves go all out on occasions, but Johnny does it differently. The game never becomes grim to him. He really enjoys himself, and in so doing gives enjoyment to others.

Good luck, Johnny, and here's wishing you a few more years in the game yet and a very successful testimonial.

Arthur Clues, Hunslet, Leeds and Australia

A really great footballer

Johnny Hunter was a rugby union schoolboy star at the famous St Joseph College, Hunters Hill, N.S.W. before joining my club, Eastern Suburbs, Sydney. Being his first rugby league captain, I feel I can add my tribute to a really great footballer. Johnny starred both as full-back and centre with Easts, and his ability was quickly recognised by officials. He went to Huddersfield unknown and on my recommendation, and I am sure that club has every reason to be proud of his achievements whilst representing them both on and off the field. Had he stayed in Australia he, without doubt, would have worn the green and gold of Australia.

Congratulations Johnny for a job well done for Australia and for the rugby league code. I know I speak for all Australians when I say, "Best wishes for every success in your future life." Good luck and God bless.

Ray Stehr

(Australian international, toured England 1933–34 & 1937–38)

"Don't kick to Hunter"

To be permitted to write a few words about Huddersfield's famous full-back, Johnny Hunter, is indeed an honour. I had the pleasure of playing with him in his first game and it was apparent even then that Huddersfield had hit the jack-pot once again. His catching of a ball was, and still is, something to marvel at. To describe his attacking qualities I can do no better than quote the words of some of Fartown's opponents, "Whatever you do don't kick the ball to Hunter." This, I contend, is the highest praise possible for any full-back.

Johnny has been one of the game's personalities and I sincerely hope that Huddersfield's R.L. followers will rally round and make this a bumper testimonial.

Alex Fiddes (former Fartown captain)

Thank you, Huddersfield

Every young lad has an ambition in life which he would like to fulfil, and one of my ambitions was to see England and my relations in Shetland. I became very pally with a chap called Lionel Cooper, in fact we started off as professional footballers with the same team.

Now this chap Cooper was becoming well known in both Aussie and England – a few English clubs were very anxious to sign him, but Lionel, being the shy type, wanted a companion. That's where I came in. The only snag was that the clubs were not prepared to sign Hunter, being an unknown. Anyhow Huddersfield did take the gamble and sign us. So my schoolboy ambition was fulfilled thanks to both Lionel and the H.C. & AC.

Of memories on the field I have plenty, and many matches stick in my mind. The first one I played in England at Hull KR. it was so cold that even the goalposts had goose pimples. The match, Other Nationalities versus France, at Hull, could have been a battle in "No Man's Land." A game against St. Helens at Fartown one Easter Monday, and the match against Hunslet when I scored after a length-of-the-field run. Of course there is the memory that every rugby league footballer will treasure, that Challenge Cup day at Wembley, especially as we were presented with winners' medals.

I do consider myself very fortunate to have played with such a great club as Huddersfield, for many reasons. I have met and played with some of the best sportsmen in the world. I wish to take this opportunity of thanking my team mates for all they have done and are doing on my behalf. The success and honours which I have enjoyed on the football field have been due to their co-operation and unselfish play. They are and have been a grand set of fellows and I am proud indeed to be associated with each and every one of them.

To the club officials and members of the Fartown Supporters' Club, and to all Huddersfield rugby league enthusiasts, I thank you for the wonderful support you have given me. On behalf of my wife and family I would like to take this opportunity of thanking the people of Huddersfield for the way they have made us welcome and when we return to Australia we will take with us some happy memories of a very friendly town.

Johnny Hunter

Lithgow Workman's 1957 team – Pat Devery's last club.
Back: Alex Kirkland, John Warfield, Jack Welch, Peter Glendenning, Peter
Evans, Bruce Henny; front: Graham Campbell, Col Hughes, Barry Sedgman,
Ted Murphy, Leo O'Brien, Ron Case., Pat Devery (captain-coach); ball boy Brian
Conran. (Courtesy Barry Staines)

Pat Devery and Russ Pepperell at Fartown in 1998.
(Courtesy *Huddersfield Examiner*)

13. Hall of Fame – and retirement

Pat Devery retired in 1954 due to a groin injury. In appreciation of the services rendered to the Fartown club and to the game by Pat Devery during his stay in England, the members and committee of the Huddersfield Supporters Club presented him with an illuminated address on 2 August 1954, before he sailed for Sydney from Tilbury on the SS Orontes on 11 August.

Back in Australia, Devery settled in the Sydney suburb of Manly and had an operation on his pelvis to find the cause of pain after physical exertion. It was found that the muscles had attached themselves to the scar tissue from the operation he had in Huddersfield, once repaired he had no further troublesome pain and was appointed non-playing coach with the Manly-Warringah club in 1955 and 1956.

He took them to the play-offs in 1955 – they finished the regular season in third place in the table – but were beaten 14–12 by eventual winners South Sydney in the semi-finals. In 1956 Manly finished sixth in the table.

The following year Devery left Manly and joined Lithgow, a mining town located west of the Blue Mountains in New South Wales, as player-coach. In 1961 he migrated to the United States after a brief period in England. He settled and taught in Boston until 1967 when he took up a teaching position in Puerto Rico where he was vice-principal of a school for children of members of the US Naval base there.

He stayed in Puerto Rico for 14 years before he retired and moved to the Pacific North West; he settled in Portland in Oregon.

On Wednesday 1 April 1998, there was clearly a hint of sadness in the voices of Pat Devery and Russ Pepperell as they stepped on to the famous Fartown field prior to the Huddersfield Giants' inaugural Super League game with Bradford Bulls two days later at the McAlpine Stadium.

The great Wembley Challenge Cup heroes' delight at meeting up for the first time in decades was in sharp contrast to their initial feelings on revisiting the place where they both made their names. The Fartown ground where they earned their reputation as rugby league greats was nothing more than a shell. The pitch remained, but the stands and terraces had long gone.

But, rather than reflect on the decline of the once revered venue, the legendary players had made their return to Huddersfield to celebrate a great new era in the club's history.

145

Pat Devery is inducted into the Balmain Tigers Hall of Fame, May 2008.
Back: Sean Hampstead, on behalf of his grandfather, the late Jack Hampstead,
Neil Pringle, Mick Davidson, on behalf of his brother, John Davidson;
front: Sid Ryan, Harry Bath, Pat Devery, Laurie Fagan, Bob Mara.
(Courtesy Michelle Nielsen, Balmain Tigers)

Pat Devery addresses the audience at the Balmain Tigers Hall of Fame in May
2008, alongside Harry Bath (left) and Sid Ryan (right).
(Courtesy Michelle Nielsen, Balmain Tigers)

In 2003, the Balmain Tigers team of the century was named:
Keith Barnes (c), Harry Bath, Arthur Beetson, Bob Boland, Tom Bourke, Tim Brasher, Larry Corowa, Jim Craig, Pat Devery, Ben Elias, Charles Fraser, Arthur Holloway, Arthur Patton, Wayne Pearce, Peter Provan, Steve Roach, Norm 'Latchem' Robinson (coach), Paul Sironen.

The members of the team of the century became the initial inductees to the Balmain Tigers Hall of Fame on 17 March 2005.In 2008 Devery made the trip to Australia from his home in Portland and was honoured as a special guest at the Tigers Centenary Dinner.

The Australian *Encyclopaedia of Rugby League Players,* compiled by Alan Whiticker and Glen Hudson, says that Devery was "One of the all-time great five-eighths" and that he was "as versatile as he was gifted." In 38 games for Balmain he scored 193 points, and over 1,000 in his time in English rugby league.

In July 1955, Lionel Cooper re-affirmed his decision to retire from the game, thus bringing a notable career to a conclusion. There were no greater connoisseurs of wing threequarter play anywhere in the world than Fartown – how could it be otherwise when from the days of the pre-World War One 'Team of All Talents' with Rosenfeld and Moorhouse as the flanks, right up to the heady days of the late 1940 to the mid–1950s the side never lacked a man or men ranking with the fastest and cleverest in the game.

Cooper was, of course, in this Huddersfield tradition, and ever since his debut in January 1947 gave his best to the delight of crowds home and away.

He made 336 appearances for the Fartowners – his try aggregate of 420 is still a longstanding Huddersfield club record for tries in a career, added to which he kicked 42 goals for a total of 1,344 points.

It is a moot point whether he or his equally brilliant fellow countryman Brian Bevan of Warrington gave the fans their greatest scoring thrills. Since the Second World War both men consistently remained two of rugby league's most magnetic attractions; both on occasion threatened the individual try-scoring record of 80 in a season, set in 1913–14 by Rosenfeld, but to date that mammoth figure remains inviolate.

After retiring from playing at Huddersfield, Cooper tried his hand at coaching with Dewsbury in the 1956–57 season. Dewsbury had declined since their success during the Second World War, when Eddie Waring was their manager and signed guest players to strengthen the side. In 1947 they had been runners-up in the championship, but were now struggling. The official club history says that "The club again faced worrying times and a change of coach seemed to be the answer. The coach was named as the famous Australian international winger Lionel Cooper... He had retired in 1955 and it was thought that his ability and knowledge of rugby league at the highest level would lead Dewsbury from the doldrums. Such aspirations were decimated. The club won only 22 matches in the following four seasons put together." In 1956–57 the club finished next to bottom of the league and won only five games.

Cooper then returned to Australia where he worked as an area manager for the AMPOL Petroleum Company – aided by his experience in a similar capacity in England – at Parkes, located in the Central West area of New South Wales at the crossroads of the Newell Highway connecting Brisbane and Melbourne.

Lionel Cooper passed away, aged 65, in Cherrybrook, a suburb of Sydney on 26 May 1987.

Hunter secured a passage booked in accordance with the Australian immigration scheme on the SS Orcades which sailed from Tilbury on 15 April 1957. He settled in the small town of Windang, now a suburb of Wollongong in New South Wales on the southern tip of the peninsula guarding the ocean entrance to Lake Illawarra.

He was employed as a carpet salesman, as he had been in Huddersfield, at Port Kembla, and played out the rest of the 1957 season with the Port Kembla Rugby League Club – the 'Blacks' – in the Illawarra League.

He was captain-coach in the 1958 Port Kembla team which went on to win the Premiership beating Western Suburbs 10–8, but missed the Grand Final because of injury – former Kangaroo Noel Mulligan took over as captain-coach. Incidentally, the Port Kembla club created a record by winning the 1958 First, Reserve and Third Grade Premierships.

Hunter's last season of football in 1958 was with the Shellharbour Rugby League club after which he hung up his boots.

A humorous anecdote to Hunter's rugby story was highlighted by his son Glenn: Hunter and John 'Whacka' Graves, 'the man who knocked dad's eye out of his head', during the Huddersfield-Australia tour game at Fartown in 1948, became great mates.

Graves, who settled in Bowral – a great potato growing area in the hinterland of the New South Wales south coast – often travelled to

Wollongong on business and 'always dropped in on dad with a bag of spuds!'

He was forced to give up his sales job due to a hearing problem and worked for a short time in the steel industry making steel pipes before becoming the postmaster at Windang – a position he held until his untimely death at the age of 54 on 1 April 1980.

After Hunter had passed away, his family wished him to be remembered in his adopted Huddersfield, and via the Huddersfield Rugby League Club Players Association, donated money to be used in some form for a memorial of Johnny.

It was decided to pass the donation on to the Huddersfield and District Cricket League who, from 1988 to 1995, introduced 'The Johnny Hunter Awards' given to 'First Eleven cricketers securing the highest individual score and best bowling analysis'.

From 1996 these became the 'Johnny Hunter Rose Bowls' for 'The First and Second Elevens cricketer respectively securing the match-winning performance of the season for his side', something, no doubt, of which Johnny would have approved.

Since 1895, hundreds of players have donned the famous claret and gold and played a major part in the club's rich history, and were recognised as such when the Huddersfield Rugby League Club Players Association inaugurated the Huddersfield Hall of Fame on 22 April 1999.

An initial 21 Fartown greats were chosen for the Hall of Fame – located at the Galpharm Stadium, the home of Huddersfield Giants. The impact the 'Team of All Talents' made on the game was reflected in the fact that Harold Wagstaff, Douglas Clark, Albert Rosenfeld and Ben Gronow were included, with the 1950s well represented by David Valentine, Jeff Bawden, Russ Pepperell, Lionel Cooper, Johnny Hunter, Pat Devery, Frank Dyson, Peter Ramsden and Ted Slevin.

The list was completed by the club's first captain Harry Lodge, Milford Sutcliffe, Alex Fiddes, Ray Markham, Len Bowkett, Don Close, Tommy Smales and Ken Senior.

'Legend' is a word which is used too much today, but these players were the genuine article. And the three 'Fartown Australians' who contributed so much to the club in the late 1940s and early 1950s were appropriately included in them.

Appendix 1. Statistics and Records

Lionel Cooper

Eastern Suburbs	App	T	G	Pts
1945 to 1946	27	14	0	42

City versus Country	App	T	G	Pts
City Firsts 1946	1	0	0	0

New South Wales	App	T	G	Pts
vs Queensland 1945 to 1946	4	6	0	18
vs England 1946	2	2	0	6
Total	6	8	0	24

Australia	App	T	G	Pts
vs England 1946	3	2	0	6

Huddersfield
Debut: versus Hull Kingston Rovers at Craven Park, 15 March 1947

Position	Season	App	T	G	Pts
1rc 2lc 9lw	1946–47	12	10	0	30
1lc 41lw	1947–48	42	37	0	111
2rw 44lw	1948–49	46	60	4	188
2rw 37lw	1949–50	39	45	0	135
1rw 42lw	1950–51	43	56	14	196
39lw	1951–52	39	64	8	208
3rc 3lc 33lw	1952–53	39	47	4	149
38lw	1953–54	38	36	5	118
38lw	1954–55	38	65	7	209
Total		**336**	**420**	**42**	**1,344**

Final game: versus Workington Town at Derwent Park, 7 May 1955

Other Nationalities (14 Appearances, 13 tries)

lw	19/9/49	vs England	at Workington	won 13–7	
lw	22/10/49	vs Wales	at Abertillery	won 6–5 (try)	
lw	10/12/50	vs France	at Bordeaux	lost 16–3	
lw	31/3/51	vs Wales	at Swansea	won 27–21 (try)	
lw	11/4/51	vs England	at Wigan	won 35–10	
lw	3/11/51	vs France	at Hull	won 17–14 (3 tries)	
lw	1/12/51	vs Wales	at Abertillery	won 22–11 (try)	
lw	23/4/52	vs England	at Wigan	lost 31–18	
lw	18/10/52	vs England	at Huddersfield	won 31–12 (try)	
lw	23/11/52	vs France	at Marseilles	won 29–10 (try)	
lw	15/4/53	vs Wales	at Warrington	lost 18–16 (try)	
lw	7/10/53	vs Wales	at Bradford	won 30–5 (3 tries)	
lw	18/10/53	vs France	at Bordeaux	won 15–10	
lw	28/11/53	vs England	at Wigan	lost 22–30 (try)	

British Empire tour of France (2 appearances, 2 tries)
lw   26/5/49   vs   France   at Bordeaux lost 10–23 (try)
lw   29/5/49   vs   Pyrenees XIII at Albi won 38–12 (try)

Australasia (2 appearances, 2 tries)
lw   19/05/51   vs   Great Britain at Leeds won 23–20 (try)*
lw   17/11/54   vs   Rugby League XIII at Bradford won 25–13 (try)

Lord Derby Memorial Fund Game
Rest of the League XIII
lw   4/10/50   vs   GB 1950 Tourists at Wigan lost 16–23 (try)

New Zealand tour of England and Wales
British Empire XIII (1 appearance, 3 tries)
lw   23/01/52   vs   New Zealand at Chelsea won 26–2 (3 tries)

20th Anniversary of French Rugby League – Combined Nations
lw   3/01/54   vs   France at Lyons lost 15–19

* Festival of Britain game

Pat Devery

Balmain	App	T	G	Pts
1944 to 1947	38	25	59	193

City vs Country	App	T	G	Pts
City Firsts 1946 and 1947	2	4	1	14

New South Wales	App	T	G	Pts
vs Queensland 1946 to 1947	6	4	3	18
vs England 1946	1	0	0	0

Australia	App	T	G	Pts
vs England 1946	3	0	0	0

Huddersfield

Debut: versus Workington Town at Derwent Park, 4 October 1947

Position	Season	App	T	G	Pts
23lc 11so	1947–48	34	18	16	86
1rc 27lc 12so	1948–49	40	20	40	140
1fb 2rc 34lc	1949–50	37	24	26	124
17lc	1950–51	17	6	21	60
22lc	1951–52	22	7	42	105
43lc	1952–53	43	16	142	332
2rc 27lc 1so	1953–54	30	7	114	249
Totals		**223**	**98**	**401**	**1,096**

Final game: versus Batley, at Mount Pleasant, 27 March 1954

Other Nationalities (11 appearances, 5 tries, 16 goals)

so	19/9/49	vs England	at Workington	won 13–7 (goal)
lc	22/10/49	vs Wales	at Abertillery	won 6–5
lc	15/1/50	vs France	at Marseilles	lost 8–3
lc	11/4/51	vs England	at Wigan	won 35–10 (try, 5g)
lc	3/11/51	vs France	at Hull	won 17–14 (4g)
lc	1/12/51	vs Wales	at Abertillery	won 22–11 (2t, goal)
lc	18/10/52	vs England	at Huddersfield	won 31–12 (3g)
lc	23/11/52	vs France	at Marseilles	won 29–10 (try)
lc	15/4/53	vs Wales	at Warrington	lost 18–16
lc	7/10/53	vs Wales	at Bradford	won 30–5 (try, 2g)
lc	28/11/53	vs England	at Wigan	lost 30–22

British Empire Tour of France (2 appearances, 3 tries, 2 goals)

lc	26/5/49	vs France	at Bordeaux	lost 23–10 (2g)
lc	29/5/49	vs Pyrenees XIII	at Albi	won 38–12 (3t)

Australasia (Festival of Britain Game)

lc	19/5/51	vs Great Britain at Leeds		won 23–20

United Kingdom XIII

rc	3/5/51	vs French XIII	at Paris	won 13–10

Johnny Hunter

Eastern Suburbs	App	T	G	Pts
1945 and 1946	21	5	0	15

Huddersfield

Debut: versus Hull Kingston Rovers at Craven Park, 15 March 1947

Position	Season	App	T	G	Pts
12fb 3rc 1lc	1946–47	16	2	0	6
28fb	1947–48	28	4	1	14
33fb 1rc	1948–49	34	13	1	41
36fb	1949–50	36	10	0	30
28fb	1950–51	28	11	0	33
26fb	1951–52	26	5	0	15
36fb	1952–53	36	1	0	3
35fb	1953–54	35	5	0	15
21fb 2rc 8lc 1lw	1954–55	32	3	1	11
10fb 3rw 3rc 15lw	1955–56	31	13	0	39
2fb 2rw 16rc 3lc 7lw	1956–57	30	7	0	21
Totals		**332**	**74**	**3**	**228**

Final game: versus Warrington, at Fartown, 13 April 1957

Other Nationalities (8 appearances)

fb	22/10/49	vs	Wales	at Abertillery	won 6–5
fb	15/1/50	vs	France	at Marseilles	lost 8–3
fb	11/4/51	vs	England	at Wigan	won 35–10
fb	3/11/51	vs	France	at Hull	won 17–14
fb	1/12/51	vs	Wales	at Abertillery	won 22–11
fb	23/4/52	vs	England	at Wigan	lost 31–18
fb	18/10/52	vs	England	at Huddersfield	won 31–12
fb	23/11/52	vs	France	at Marseilles	won 29–10

British Empire XIII (2 appearances, 4 goals)

fb	26/5/49	vs France	at Bordeaux	lost 10–23
fb	19/5/51	vs Wales	at Llanelli	won 29–16 (4g)
	(Festival of Britain Game)			

Key

fb	full back
rw	right wing
rc	right centre
lc	left centre
lw	left wing
so	stand–off half

Appendix 2. Top try, goal and point scorers

Seasons when a Huddersfield player was in the national top try, goal and point scorers.

1947–48

Tries
1. 57 B Bevan (Warrington)
2. 49 WG Ratcliffe (Wigan)
3. **37 LW Cooper (Huddersfield)**
15. **22 J Anderson (Huddersfield)**

Goals
1. 141 EH Ward (Wigan)
2. **102 J Bawden (Huddersfield)**
3. 96 AJ Risman (Workington T)

Points
1. 312 EH Ward (Wigan)
2. **261 J Bawden (Huddersfield)**
3. 206 H Palin (Warrington)
16. **111 LW Cooper (Huddersfield)**

1948–49

Tries
1. **60 LW Cooper (Huddersfield)**
2. 56 B Bevan (Warrington)
3. 36 GW Ratcliffe (Wigan)
15. **20 PC Devery (Huddersfield)**

Goals
1. 155 EH Ward (Wigan)
2. 149 H Palin (Warrington)
3. **103 J Bawden (Huddersfield)**
20. **40 PC Devery (Huddersfield)**

Points
1. 361 EH Ward (Wigan)
2. 322 H Palin (Warrington)
3. 221 J Bawden (Huddersfield)
4. **188 LW Cooper (Huddersfield)**
9. **140 PC Devery (Huddersfield)**

1949–50

Tries
1. 57 BC Nordgren (Wigan)
2. **46 LW Cooper (Huddersfield)**
3. 36 AH Daniels (Halifax)
6. **32 R Cracknell (Huddersfield)**
12. **24 PC Devery (Huddersfield)**

Goals
1. 133 K Gee (Wigan)
2. 133 H Palin (Warrington)
3. 115 HE Cook (Leeds)
8. **93 J Bawden (Huddersfield)**

Points
1. 290 H Palin (Warrington)
2. 284 K Gee (Wigan)
3. 245 HE Cook (Leeds)
7. **213 J Bawden (Huddersfield)**
19. **138 LW Cooper (Huddersfield)**

154

1950–51

Tries
1. 68 B Bevan (Warrington)
2. **59 LW Cooper (Huddersfield)**
3. 42 BC Nordgren (Wigan)

Points
1. 322 HE Cook (Leeds)
2. 281 J Perry (Batley)
3. 237 AJ Risman (Workington T)
6. **205 LW Cooper (Huddersfield)**

Huddersfield did not have a player in the top 20 goalkickers.

1951–52

Tries
1. **71 LW Cooper (Huddersfield)**
2. 63 J McLean (Bradford N)
3. 52 F Castle (Barrow)
6. **47 R Cracknell (Huddersfield)**
10. **31 P Henderson (Huddersfield)**

Points
1. 313 W Horne (Barrow)
2. 308 J Phillips (Bradford N)
3. 297 JA Ledgard (Leigh)
6. **229 LW Cooper Huddersfield)**

Huddersfield did not have a player in the top 20 goalkickers.

1952–53

Tries
1. 72 B Bevan (Warrington)
2. 59 J McLean (Bradford N)
3. **50 LW Cooper (Huddersfield)**
4. 47 BC Nordgren (Wigan)
5. **46 P Henderson (Huddersfield)**

Goals
1. 170 H Bath (Warrington)
2. 149 G Langfield (St Helens)
3. **145 PC Devery (Huddersfield)**

Points
1. 379 H Bath (Warrington)
2. **341 PC Devery (Huddersfield)**
3. 322 G Langfield (St Helens)
20. **158 LW Cooper (Huddersfield)**

1953–54

Tries
1. 67 B Bevan (Warrington)
2. 52 J McLean (Bradford N)
3. 41 A Turnbull (Leeds)
4. **40 LW Cooper (Huddersfield)**
9. **32 P Henderson (Huddersfield)**

Goals
1. 153 P Metcalfe (St Helens)
2. 153 H Bath (Warrington)
3. 143 J Phillips (Bradford N)
9. **116 PC Devery (Huddersfield)**

Points
1. 369 P Metcalfe (St Helens)
2. 318 H Bath (Warrington)
3. 310 J Phillips (Bradford N)
7. 256 PC Devery (Huddersfield)

1954–55

Tries
1. 66 LW Cooper (Huddersfield)
2. 63 B Bevan (Warrington)
3. 45 P Henderson (Huddersfield)

Points
1. 374 JA Ledgard (Leigh)
2. 264 H Bath (Warrington)
3. 247 BL Jones (Leeds)
8. 212 LW Cooper Huddersfield)

Huddersfield did not have a player in the top 20 goalkickers.

Appendix 3. Huddersfield league records

Season	Place	Pl	W	D	L	F	A	Pts	
1946–47:	7	36	24	2	10	572	332	50	
1947–48:	3	36	26	2	8	669	240	54	
1948–49:	3	36	27	0	9	626	290	54	
1949–50:	2	36	28	1	7	694	362	57	
1950–51:	9	36	20	2	14	575	410	42	
1951–52:	4	36	26	0	10	785	446	52	
1952–53:	4	36	27	2	7	747	366	56	
1953–54:	6	36	24	0	12	689	417	48	
1954–55:	11	36	22	0	14	790	483	44	
1955–56:	14	36	18	1	17	606	544	37	51.37%
1956–57:	9	38	23	0	15	667	533	46	

In 1955–56 the league places were decided on percentages due to Belle Vue's withdrawal from the competition.

Appendix 4. Other Nationalities match details

Matches that included Lionel Cooper, Pat Devery or Johnny Hunter.

1949–50

England 7 Other Nationalities 13
Workington 19 September 1949
England: J.A. Ledgard (Leigh), J. Lawrenson (Workington T), E. Kerwick (Leigh),
E.J. Ashcroft (Wigan), G. Clark (Dewsbury), W. Horne (Barrow), T. Bradshaw (Wigan),
D. Naughton (Widnes), J. Egan (Wigan), J. Hayton (Workington T), J.J. Featherstone
(Warrington), C. Armitt (Swinton), W.H. Ivison (Workington T).
Scorers: Try: Clark. Goals: Ledgard 2.
Other Nationalities: G. Wilson (Huddersfield) B. Bevan ((Warrington), A.H. Paskins
(Workington T, R. Bartlett (Leeds), **L.W. Cooper (Huddersfield), P.C. Devery
(Huddersfield),** D. Jackson (Hull), R.E. McMaster (Leeds) K.H. Kearney (Leeds),
J.S. Pansegrouw (Halifax), A.H. Bath (Warrington), J.R. Mudge (Workington T),
D.D. Valentine (Huddersfield).
Scorers: Tries: Bevan 2, G. Wilson. Goals: Devery, Bath.
Referee: Charlie Appleton (Warrington)
Attendance: 17,576

Wales 5 Other Nationalities 6
Abertillery 22 October 1949
Wales: S. Williams (Salford), A.H. Daniels (Halifax), J.B. Mahoney (Dewsbury), N. Harris
(Leigh), L. Williams (Hunslet), J. Davies (Salford), W.M. Banks (Huddersfield), T. Danter
(Hull), F. Osmond (Swinton), E. Hawkins (Salford), T.J.F. Foster (Bradford N),
W.J.D. Howes (Wakefield T), B.V. Goldswain (Oldham).
Scorer: Try: Davies. Goal: Davies.
Other Nationalities: **J.C.H Hunter (Huddersfield),** B. Bevan (Warrington), A.H.
Paskins (Workington T), **P.C. Devery (Huddersfield), L.W. Cooper Huddersfield),**
C.R. Mountford (Wigan), D. Jackson (Hull), R.E. McMaster (Leeds), K.H. Kearney
(Leeds), A.H. Bath (Warrington), A. Clues (Leeds), J. Payne (Hull), D.D. Valentine
(Huddersfield).
Scorers: Tries: Bevan, Cooper.
Referee: Charlie Appleton (Warrington)
Attendance: 2,000

France 8 Other Nationalities 3
Marseilles 15 January 1950
France: Puig-Aubert, V.Cantoni (Toulouse), G.Comes (Perpignan), P.Dejean (Perpignan),
R.Contrastin(Bordeaux), C.Galaup (Albi), R.Duffort (Lyons), A. Ulma (Perpignan),
G. Genoud (Villeneuve), A. Beraud(Marseilles), H.Berthomieu(Marseilles), E. Brousse
(Lyons), R.Perez (Marseilles).
Scorers: Tries: Contrastin 2. Goal: Dejean.
Other Nationalities: **J.C.H. Hunter (Huddersfield),** R. Bartlett (Leeds), A.H. Paskins
(Workington T), **P.C. Devery (Huddersfield),** B.C. Nordgren (Wigan), C.R. Mountford
(Wigan), D. Jackson (Hull), R.E. McMaster (Leeds), K.H. Kearney (Leeds), J.C. Daly
(Huddersfield), A. Clues (Leeds), R.S. Robson (Huddersfield), D.D. Valentine
(Huddersfield).
Scorer: Try: Bartlett.
Referee: M. Guidicelli.
Attendance: 20,000

1950–51

France 16 Other Nationalities 3
Bordeaux 10 December 1950
France: Puig-Aubert, V. Cantoni, J. Crespo, Y. Treilhes, R. Contrastin, C. Galoup,
R. Duffort L. Mazon, M. Martin, A. Beraud, E. Ponsinet, E. Brousse, G. Calixte
Scorers: Tries: Crespo, Mazon. Goals: Puig Aubert 5.
Other Nationalities: H.E. Cook (Leeds), B. Bevan (Warrington), R. Bartlett (Leeds),
I.W. Clark (Huddersfield), **L.W. Cooper (Huddersfield),** C.R. Mountford (Wigan),
D. Jackson (Hull), R.E. McMaster (Leeds), A.H. Bath (Warrington), J.C. Daly
(Huddersfield), A.C. Clues (Leeds), J.R. Mudge (Workington T), D.D. Valentine
(Huddersfield).
Scorer: Try: Bevan.
Referee: M. Vacher (Lyons)
Attendance: 28,000.

Wales 21 Other Nationalities 27
Swansea 31 March 1951
Wales: J. Evans (Hunslet), R. Lambert (Dewsbury), D. Gullick (St Helens), L. Williams
(Hunslet), T. Cook (Halifax), R. Williams (Leeds), W.M. Banks (Huddersfield), D. Harris
(Castleford), F.F. Osmond (Swinton), M. Ford (Aberavon), G. Parsons (St Helens),
R. Gale (St Helens), G. James (Hunslet).
Scorers: Tries: Cook 2, Gullick, Ford, James. Goals: Evans 3.
Other Nationalities: H.E. Cook (Leeds), B. Bevan (Warrington), T. Allan (Leigh),
A.H. Paskins (Workington T), **L.W. Cooper (Huddersfield),** P. Henderson
(Huddersfield), I. Proctor (Leeds), J.R. Mudge (Workington T) K. Kearney (Leeds),
J.C. Daly (Huddersfield), A.C. Clues (Leeds), R. Robson (Salford), D.D. Valentine
(Huddersfield).
Scorers: Tries: Bevan, Allan, Paskins, Cooper, Henderson, Proctor, Clues. Goals: Cook 3.
Referee: A.S. Dobson (Pontefract)
Attendance: 5,000

England 10 Other Nationalities 35
Wigan 11 April 1951
England: J. Cunliffe (Wigan), G.WE. Ratcliffe (Wigan), E.J. Ashcroft (Wigan), E. Gibson
(Workington T), G. Clark (Dewsbury), K. Dean (Halifax), T. Bradshaw (Wigan), K. Gee
(Wigan) A. Wood (Featherstone R), F. Barton (Wigan), G. Palmer (Batley), N. Silcock
(Wigan), W. Ivison (Workington T).
Scorers: Tries: Cunliffe, Ratcliffe. Goals: Dean 2.
Other Nationalities: **J.C.H Hunter (Huddersfield),** B. Bevan (Warrington), T. Allan
(Leigh), **P.C. Devery (Huddersfield), L.W. Cooper (Huddersfield),** C.R. Mountford
(Wigan), D. Jackson (Hull), J.C. Daly (Huddersfield), T. McKinney (Salford), J.R. Mudge
(Workington T), A.H. Bath (Warrington), R. Robson (Salford), D.D. Valentine
(Huddersfield).
Scorers: Tries: Bevan 3, Daly, Mudge, Valentine. Goals: Devery 5, Bath 2.
Referee: M. Coates (Pudsey)
Attendance: 16,860.

1951–52

Other Nationalities 17 France 14
Hull 3 November 1951
Other Nationalities: **J.C.H. Hunter (Huddersfield),** B. Bevan (Warrington),
A. Paskins (Workington T), **P.C. Devery (Huddersfield), L.W. Cooper
(Huddersfield),** P. Henderson (Huddersfield), C. Kelly (Rochdale H),
R.E. McMaster (Leeds), T McKinney (Salford), J.R. Mudge (Workington T),
A.C. Clues (Leeds), G. Burke (Leigh), D.D. Valentine (Huddersfield).
Scorers: Tries: Cooper 3. Goals: Devery 4.
France: Puig-Aubert (Carcassonne), J. Merquey (Marseilles), G. Comes (Perpignan),
V. Cantoni (Toulouse), R. Duffort (Paris Celtic), J. Crespo (Lyons),
L. Mazon (Carcassonne), M. Martin (Carcassonne), P. Bartoletti (Bordeaux),
E. Brousse (Paris Celtic), E. Poncinet (Carcassonne), F. Metropolis (Lyons).
Scorers: Tries: Cantoni, Bartoletti. Goals: Puig Aubert 4.
Referee: G.S. Phillips (Widnes)
Attendance: 18,000

Wales 11 Other Nationalities 22
Abertillery 1 December 1951
Wales: J. Evans (Hunslet): M. Hunt (Cardiff), L. Williams (Hunslet), V.J. Harrison
(St Helens), T. Cook (Halifax), R. Williams (Leeds), W.M. Banks (Huddersfield), O. Phillips
(Swinton), F. Osmond (Swinton), E. Gwyther (Belle Vue R), D. Phillips (Belle Vue R),
E.H. Ward (Cardiff), R. Cale (St Helens).
Scorers: Tries: Hunt, L. Williams, R. Williams. Goal: Ward.
Other Nationalities: **J.C.H. Hunter (Huddersfield),** B. Bevan (Warrington), A. Paskins
(Workington T), **P.C. Devery (Huddersfield), L.W. Cooper (Huddersfield),**
P. Henderson (Huddersfield), C. Kelly (Rochdale Hornets), J. Burke (Leigh), T. McKinney
(Salford), J.R. Mudge (Workington T), A.C. Clues (Leeds), A.H. Bath (Warrington),
D.D. Valentine (Huddersfield)
Scorers: Tries: Bevan 2, Devery 2, Cooper. Goals: Devery, Bath.
Referee: Charlie Appleton (Warrington)
Attendance: 3,386

England 31 Other Nationalities 18
Wigan 23 April 1952
England: J.A. Ledgard (Leigh), R. Cracknell (Huddersfield), D. Greenall (St Helens),
E. Ward (Bradford N), F.H. Castle (Barrow), W. Horne (Barrow), A.E. Toohey (Barrow),
A.G. Prescott (St Helens), A. Ackerley (Halifax), F. Barton (Wigan), N. Silcock (Wigan),
C.H. Pawsey (Leigh), W.H. Ivison (Workington T).
Scorers: Tries: Cracknell 2, Castle 2, Horne, Greenall, Ledgard.
Goals: Horne 3, Ledgard 2.
Other Nationalities: **J.C.H. Hunter (Huddersfield),** B. Bevan (Warrington),
A. Paskins (Workington T), T. Allan (Leigh), **L.W. Cooper (Huddersfield),**
L.E. Verrenkamp (Leeds), C. Kelly (Rochdale H), R. McMaster (Leeds), T. McKinney
(Salford), A.H. Bath (Warrington), A.C. Clues (Leeds), J.R. Mudge (Workington T),
D.D. Valentine (Huddersfield).
Scorers: Tries: Bevan 2, Allan 2. Goals: Bath 3.
Referee: T. Armitage (Huddersfield)
Attendance: 19,785

159

1952–53

England versus Other Nationalities

Huddersfield 18 October 1952

England: J.A. Ledgard (Leigh), J. Lewthwaite (Barrow), R. Ryder (Warrington), E. Ward (Bradford N), F. Castle (Barrow), K. Dean (Halifax), E. Toohey (Barrow), A.G. Prescott (St Helens), A. Ackerley (Halifax), M. Scott (Hull), C.H. Pawsey (Leigh), R. Ryan (Warrington), W. Blan (Wigan).

Scorers: Tries: Lewthwaite, Pawsey. Goals: Ledgard.

Other Nationalities: **J.C.H. Hunter (Huddersfield),** B. Bevan (Warrington), A.H. Paskins (Workington T**), P.C. Devery (Huddersfield), L.W. Cooper (Huddersfield),** P. Henderson (Huddersfield), C.R. Kelly (Wigan), J.C. Daly (Featherstone R), T. McKinney (Workington T), J.R. Mudge (Workington T), A.H. Bath (Warrington), A.C. Clues (Leeds), D.D. Valentine (Huddersfield).

Scorers: Tries: Bevan 4, Henderson 2, Cooper. Goals: Devery 3, Bath 2.

Referee: Ron Gelder (Wakefield).

France 10 Other Nationalities 29

Marseilles 23 November 1952

France: Puig Aubert, M. Bellan, R. Rey, J. Merquey, O. Lespes, G. Benausse, C. Teisseire, F. Rinaldi, M. Martin, P. Bartoletti, H. Berthomieu, G. Delaye, R. Perez.

Scorers: Tries: Merquey 2. Goals: Puig Aubert 2.

Other Nationalities: **J.C.H. Hunter (Huddersfield),** B. Bevan (Warrington), T.W. Lynch (Halifax), **P.C. Devery (Huddersfield), L.W. Cooper (Huddersfield),** P. Henderson (Huddersfield), C. Kelly (Wigan), J.C. Daly (Featherstone R), T. McKinney (Workington T), J.R. Mudge (Workington T), A.C. Clues (Leeds), A.H. Bath (Warrington), D.D. Valentine (Huddersfield).

Scorers: Tries: Bevan 2, Devery, Cooper, Henderson, Kelly, Valentine. Goals: Bath 4. Attendance: 17,611.

Other Nationalities versus Wales

Warrington 15 April 1953

Other Nationalities: J. Phillips (Bradford N), B. Bevan (Warrington), T. Allan (Leigh), **P.C. Devery (Huddersfield), L.W. Cooper (Huddersfield),** C.R. Mountford (Warrington), N Black (Keighley), J.C. Daly (Featherstone R), W. Ellean (Rochdale H), J.R. Mudge (Workington T), A.H. Bath (Warrington), A.C. Clues (Leeds), D.D. Valentine (Huddersfield).

Scorers: Tries: Cooper, Black, Clues, Valentine. Goals: Bath 2.

Wales: J. Evans (Hunslet), D.R. Bevan (Wigan), L. Williams (Hunslet), N. Harris (Rochdale H), T. Cook (Halifax), K. Williams (Leeds), W.M. Banks (Huddersfield), M. Condon (Halifax), P.T. Harris (Hull), E. Gwyther (Leeds), G. Parsons (St Helens), C. Winslade (Oldham), G. James (Hunslet).

Scorers: Tries: L. Williams, N. Harris, P.T. Harris, Parsons. Goals: Evans 3.

Referee: A. Hill (Dewsbury)

Attendance: 8,449

1953–54

Other Nationalities versus Wales

Bradford 7 October 1953

Other Nationalities: J. Phillips (Bradford N), B. Bevan (Warrington), A. Paskins (Workington T), **P.C. Devery (Huddersfield), L.W. Cooper (Huddersfield),** J.G. Robinson (York), N. Black (Keighley), B. Wilson (Workington T), W. Ellean (Rochdale H), J.R. Mudge (Workington T), A.C. Clues (Leeds), A.H. Bath (Warrington), D.D. Valentine (Huddersfield).

Scorers: Tries: Cooper 3, Bevan, Devery, Ellean. Goals: Phillips 4, Devery 2.

Wales: J. Evans (Hunslet) goal, S. Llewellyn (St Helens), L. Williams (Hunslet), D. Gullick (St Helens), A.H. Daniels (Halifax), R. Williams (Leeds) try, W.M. Banks (Huddersfield), G.M. Thorley (Halifax), P.T. Harris (Hull), W.E. Hopper (Leeds), G. Parsons (St Helens), M. Tiernay (Belle Vue R), B.V. Goldswain (Oldham)

Scorers: Try: R. Williams. Goal: Evans.

Referee: C.F. Appleton (Warrington)

France versus Other Nationalities

Bordeaux

France: Puig-Aubert (Perpignan), M. Voron (Lyons), C. Teisseire (Carcasonne), A. Carrere (Bordeaux), R. Contrastin (Bordeaux), J. Merquey (Marseilles), J. Crespo (Lyons), A. Carrere (Villeneuve), J. Audoubert (Lyons), F. Rinaldi (Marseilles), R. Bernard (Albi), E. Poncinet (Carcasonne), R. Guilhem (Carcasonne)

Scorers: Tries: Voron, Contrastin. Goals: Puig-Aubert.

Other Nationalities: J. Phillips (Bradford N) 3 goals, B. Bevan (Warrington) 2 tries, A. Paskins (Workington T), T.W. Lynch (Halifax**), L.W. Cooper (Huddersfield),** J.G. Robinson (York), N. Black (Keighley), B. Wilson (Workington T), W. Ellean (Rochdale H), J.R. Mudge (Workington T), A.C. Clues (Leeds), R. Mossop (Leigh), D.D. Valentine (Huddersfield).

Scorers: Tries: Bevan 2, Robinson. Goals: Phillips 3.

Referee: Charlie Appleton (Warrington)

Attendance: 12,190

England versus Other Nationalities

Wigan 23 November 1953

England: E. Cahill (Rochdale H), P. Norburn (Swinton), D. Greenall (St Helens), E. Gibson (Workington T), F. Castle (Barrow), W. Horne (Barrow), S. Kielty (Halifax), A.G. Prescott (St Helens), H. Bradshaw (Dewsbury), J. Wilkinson (Halifax), C. Pawsey (Leigh), B. Watts (York), K. Traill (Bradford N).

Scorers: Tries: Norburn 4, Gibson, Castle, Traill. Goals: Horne 3.

Other Nationalities: J. Phillips (Bradford N), B. Bevan (Warrington), A. Paskins (Workington T), **P.C. Devery (Huddersfield), L.W. Cooper (Huddersfield),** J.G. Robinson (York), F.R. Dawson (Workington T), B. Wilson (Workington T), W. Ellean (Rochdale H), J.R. Mudge (Workington T), A.C. Clues (Leeds), R. Mossop (Leigh), D.D. Valentine (Huddersfield)

Scorers: Tries: Bevan 2, Cooper, Robinson. Goals: Phillips 5.

Referee: G.S. Phillips (Widnes)

Attendance: 19,012

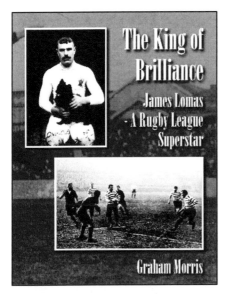

Great new book about one of the sport's genuine legends. James Lomas played for Bramley, Salford, Oldham and York, and won representative honours for Lancashire, Cumberland, England and Great Britain. He captained the first Lions team to tour Australia and New Zealand in 1910. This is the first biography of him.

Published in October 2011 at £16.95 (hardback). Copies available direct from London League Publications Ltd, PO Box 65784, London NW2 9NS (cheques payable to London League Publications Ltd); credit card orders via our website: www.llpshop.co.uk or from any bookshop

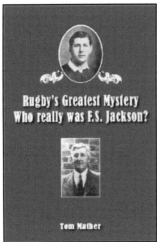

Rugby's Greatest Mystery
Who really was F.S. Jackson?

A true life rugby detective story
This is the story of a man whose life was made up of mystery, intrigue and deception, but was also a Rugby Union star before the First World War. He played for Leicester and Cornwall when they won the 1908 County Championship. He was selected for the Anglo-Welsh Rugby Union tour to New Zealand and Australia in 1908. However, the RFU recalled him from the tour and banned him from the sport over allegations that he was a professional player, and had played for Swinton in the Northern Union. The scandal around his suspension from rugby union caused great problems for the RFU and almost saw a further split in the game.

He then played Rugby League for New Zealand, against the British Lions in 1910. After the First World War he was reinstated by the New Zealand RU, became an East Coast selector and saw his son play for the All Blacks. For around 60 years he used the name Frederick Stanley Jackson, even though it was not his given name. When he died in 1957 he took to the grave his true identity. Even his family knew little about his early years in England, or even where he came from. **It was a mystery that remained unresolved until now.** The book also includes an analysis of the development of Leicester Tigers RFC up to the First World War.

Published in March 2012 at £12.95. Copies available direct from
London League Publications Ltd, PO Box 65784, London NW2 9NS
(cheques payable to London League Publications Ltd);
credit card orders via our website: www.llpshop.co.uk or from any bookshop.

Best in the Northern Union

The pioneering 1910
Rugby League Lions tour
of Australia and New Zealand

Tom Mather

Fascinating account of the first Great Britain Lions tour of Australia and New Zealand. Published in 2010 at £12.95, special offer £12.00 direct from London League Publications Ltd. Credit card orders via www.llpshop.co.uk , orders by cheque to LLP, PO Box 65784, London NW2 9NS

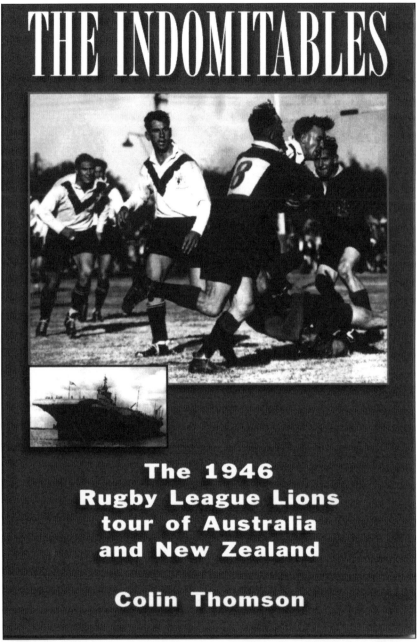

THE INDOMITABLES

**The 1946
Rugby League Lions
tour of Australia
and New Zealand**

Colin Thomson

The story of the historic 1946 Lions tour. Includes Doug Phillips' tour diary.
Published in 2009 at £12.95, special offer £12.00 direct from London League
Publications Ltd. Credit card orders via www.llpshop.co.uk , orders by cheque
to LLP, PO Box 65784, London NW2 9NS

Braver than all the rest
A mother fights for her son

Philip Howard

Dave and Sarah Burgess are devastated when their young son Karl is found to have muscular dystrophy. Then another tragedy hits the family hard. But the family are committed to do the best they can for Karl, who has a passion for rugby league. Based in Castleton, a Yorkshire town near the border with Lancashire, Karl's determination to get the most out of life, despite his disability, inspires those around him, in particular Chris Anderton, one of the Castleton Rugby League Club players, who is coming to the end of his career in the game. A moving novel of family life and rugby league.
Published in 2010 at £9.95, special offer £9.00 direct from London League Publications Ltd. Credit card orders via www.llpshop.co.uk , orders by cheque to LLP, PO Box 65784, London NW2 9NS

From grass to glass

A Rugby League Journey

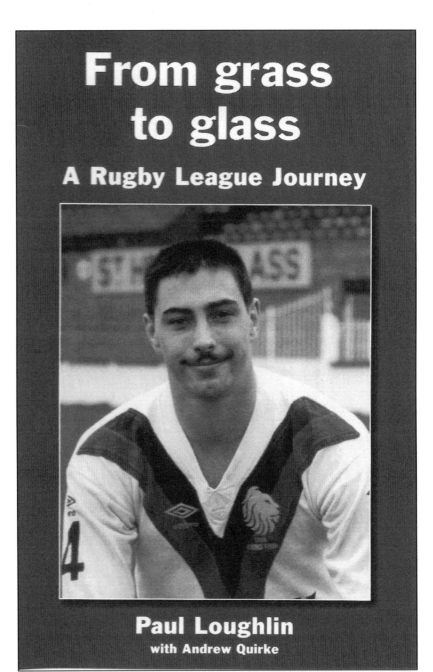

Paul Loughlin
with Andrew Quirke

Autobiography of Great Britain, St Helens, Huddersfield and Bradford Bulls
Star. Published in 2011 at £12.95, special offer £12.00 direct from London
League Publications Ltd. Credit card orders via www.llpshop.co.uk ,orders
by cheque to LLP, PO Box 65784, London NW2 9NS